Triple-O

The White Spot Story

Constance Brissenden

OPUS

Published and produced for White Spot Limited by
Opus Productions Inc.
Corporate Office: 300 West Hastings Street
Vancouver, British Columbia, Canada V6B 1K6

First published 1993

10 9 8 7 6 5 4 3 2 1

© Copyright Opus Productions Inc., 1993

All rights reserved. Without limiting the rights under copyright reserved above, no part of this publication may be reproduced, stored in or introduced into a retrieval system, or transmitted in any form or by any means (electronic, mechanical, photocopying, recording or otherwise), without the prior written permission of both the copyright owner and the above publisher of this book.

The Publishers do not assume responsibility for the historical accuracy of the information contained in this book. Photographs and artifacts have been credited wherever possible.

Canadian Cataloguing In Publication Data
Brissenden, Constance, 1947-
Triple-O: the White Spot story

Includes bibliographical references.
ISBN O-921926-11-1

1. White Spot Ltd.–History.   2. Restaurants–British Columbia–Lower Mainland–History.
I. Title.
TX945.5.W55B75 1993   647.957113'3   C93-091767-7

Project Director/Editor-in-Chief: Marthe Love
Designer: Chris Dahl, Chris Dahl Art & Design
Creative Consultant: Derik Murray
Vice President, Marketing: Glenn McPherson
Production Manager/Visual Research Coordinator: Paula Guise
Production Coordinator: Wendy Darling
Administrative Assistant: Robin Evans
Studio/Location Photography: Perry Danforth, Grant Waddell/Derik Murray Photography Inc.

Main text and sidebars written by Constance Brissenden
Captions and additional writing by Bob Sherrin
Editor and Photo Researcher: Gail Buente
Editorial Assistant: Jennifer Love
Text Researcher: Jim Oakes

Printed and bound in Canada
by Metropolitan Press Ltd.

Previous Page: To illustrate *The Wonderbird Legend,* White Spot commissioned Kwakiutl ritualistic carver Ellen Neel to create this magnificent totem pole in 1953.

Contents

7
INTRODUCTION
The Stuff That Legends Are Made Of

11
CHAPTER 1
1928 – 1938 The Hustler Years

25
CHAPTER 2
1938 – 1949 The Expansion Years

41
CHAPTER 3
1949 – 1960 The Boom Years

57
CHAPTER 4
1960 – 1982 The Transition Years

71
CHAPTER 5
1982 – 1993 Being The Best

91
EPILOGUE
The Legend Continues

94
ACKNOWLEDGEMENTS

96
BIBLIOGRAPHY

• 1960s promotional placemat highlighting White Spot locations as well as various tourist attractions in the Lower Mainland.

The Stuff That Legends Are Made Of

just say the words "White Spot" and listen to a legend 65 years in the making.

The story of this remarkable restaurant group weaves through British Columbia's history. It all started simply enough, on a slightly overcast day in June 1928 when Nat Bailey, the founder of White Spot restaurants, sold his first barbecued beef sandwich. Today, guests can dine at any one of 39 locations, including the company's first franchise in Vernon, B.C., and its first U.S. restaurant in Bellingham, Washington, a feat that would have made Nat proud. Millions of people have pulled into White Spot's drive-ins or dined at its booths inside; countless tales have been told about the great times enjoyed at "The Spot."

White Spot is also a story of many firsts: the first drive-in restaurant in Canada, the first carhop, the first aluminum tray, the first knotty pine interior (starting a trend in homes across B.C.), the first stainless steel kitchens, the first Pirate Pak. And of course, there is first love, for many a romance has blossomed over a Legendary Hamburger topped with Triple-O, the most famous sauce in North America.

• **Left:** 1936 promotional coins given to tourists at the Canada-U.S. border. **Facing page:** Icons of a bygone era evoke memories of White Spot.

When the original White Spot Barbecue opened in 1928, the province was enthralled with the energy of the Roaring Twenties. Flappers and their beaus rode in Model Ts and Vancouver was a small city with big ambitions. Today, four-wheel drive vehicles are the fashion and the little city has grown up. British Columbia is now Canada's official Gateway to the Pacific Rim, and Vancouver, with a population of 1.5 million people, is a thriving multicultural city of international stature.

As the province grew, so did White Spot. More than 60 years ago, the first 10-cent hot dogs were sold from the tiny log cabin barbecue with the white spot on its roof. Today the family restaurant has grown into one of British Columbia's largest business empires, and the restaurant group has become a household name. From Vancouver to Kelowna, Victoria to Prince George, and now in Bellingham, Washington as well, eating at White Spot continues to be a daily ritual played out from early morning breakfasts to late-night snacks. Generation after generation celebrates weekends here, and birthdays, anniversaries, Mother's Day and New Year's.

Nat Bailey had been a self-made man since he was 12 years old, hawking newspapers on the streets of Vancouver, and was only 26 when he started White Spot. Today, under the ownership of another enterprising B.C. spirit, Peter C. Toigo, White Spot plays a significant role in the economy of the province. In its auspicious 65th year, the company continues to grow, garnering acclaim throughout the restaurant industry — introducing new menu items to reflect current food trends, opening new locations and revitalizing old favourites with elegant new decors. Staff training is a top priority and service, as a result, has never been better. The company is deeply proud of its employees and their commitment to keeping the restaurant group

foremost in the hearts of its customers.

If you look around any White Spot, you'll understand why people keep coming back. Friendly smiles and warm service welcome guests time after time. At neighbouring tables, there's always a diversity of guests, enjoying their meal in relaxed comfort. On a Sunday morning, for example, at Vancouver's Kingsway and Knight St. location, a pair of teenagers in colourful vests and baggy jeans sit in a booth next to a young family with two small children. A foursome of grandparents in their best suits relax over brunch while a lone male diner checks out the real estate listings in the newspaper. White Spot has its "regulars" who have been coming back for decades, as well as a whole new crowd who keep each restaurant vital and alive. While log cabin drive-ins have given way to warm and welcoming family restaurants, the pursuit of excellence remains as White Spot has expanded to become British Columbia's leading restaurant group. Its original goals of "quality, service and consistency" persist to this day as do its enduring menu favourites — among them, fresh seasonal berry pies, Chicken in the Straw and strawberry cheesecake made from a secret recipe.

When the doors were opened recently at one of White Spot's new locations, a young couple asked the hostess rather anxiously: "Can we still get a Triple-O hamburger and a bowl of clam chowder here?" Certainly they can. Some good things never change.

Sixty-five years after White Spot opened, it's still British Columbia's favourite restaurant. *Triple-O – The White Spot Story* celebrates its remarkable history. •

• A collection of White Spot memorabilia. The familiar logo gives personality to many everyday items. *Clockwise from left:* 1955 SMILE pencil, courtesy of Erwin Jellen; 1970 logo pin, courtesy of Erwin Jellen; 1955 SMILE lighter, courtesy of Erwin Jellen; 1980 coffee mug, courtesy of Erwin Jellen; 1960s pie card, courtesy of Erwin Jellen; silver McGill change maker, courtesy of Steve Fee; 1955 logo pin, courtesy of Erwin Jellen; pie plate, courtesy of Peter Szerencsi; 1988 watch, courtesy of Erwin Jellen; 1950s menu, courtesy of R.J. Stout.

1928-1938 The Hustler Years

True heroes are often people who shy from the limelight. So it was with Nat Bailey. Growing up in the tough early years of the century, Nat barely managed a Grade 8 education. Undaunted, he became a highly successful and respected businessman, and though his first business ventures often survived through the good will of creditors and bankers, he learned the true meaning of that support by helping others to succeed. Indeed, thousands got a start in life as members of the White Spot family. Yet despite the fact that Nat loved to work, he always made time for play, particularly for his beloved baseball. From the beginning he encouraged children in the little leagues as well as professionals in the big show.

Simply put, Nat loved people. Even as a young man, he was considered a father figure to many. Bob Stout began to work for Nat in the 1930s selling peanuts at Vancouver sporting events and stayed with him for 50 years. Bob recalls, "He wasn't one to lavish praise on you, but an approving nod from him could make you feel on top of the world." Perhaps the White Spot family helped Nat Bailey feel on the top of the world, too, because within it he found the security and happiness he missed as a child.

Born January 31, 1902 in St. Paul, Minnesota, Nathaniel Ryal Bailey had his first taste of the food business early in life. For in the days before trains had dining cars, his mother was a cook and baker in railway eating houses, and his father ran wheels of fortune in carnivals across the United States. His family followed him from town to town, house to house, and hope to hope. In 1911 Nat's father thought he'd found a secure job in Vancouver, but the job did not materialize and shortly after the family's arrival, his wife fell ill. It was up to young Nat to help out.

Like his father, Nat Bailey was always willing to gamble on the future, and in 1914 this 12-year-old newcomer to a young city took to the downtown streets to hawk newspapers. Some say he went fist-to-fist with another boy for his corner spot, others that he bought out his rival; but most likely Nat simply outhustled him. By the time he hit 18, Nat was out of the newspaper business and into something close to his heart and to that of anyone who'd ever gone without: food. He was now selling popcorn and peanuts on the city streets, and he'd also combined his love of sports with a fan's love of a good ballpark frank. Nat's hot dogs, peanuts and coffee kept them shouting for more at Athletic Park.

And he could read that crowd like nobody else. A quick scan of the bleachers told him just how many bags of peanuts and how many cups of coffee he could sell. If the numbers were low, he'd send "the boys" into the crowd to extol the virtues of his

• **The originals: Nat and the Drive-in at Granville and 67th.**
Facing page: **Granville and Hastings streets in the heart of Vancouver's downtown core, 1928.**

COURTESY OF R.J. STOUT

Out to the Ballgame

everybody in town knew Nat Bailey, that personable chap whose powerful musical voice added a "Barnum and Bailey" touch to local events, first as a sports announcer, later as a seller of snack foods to Vancouver's avid sports fans. Since the early 1920s he had been a familiar figure around Athletic Park and Denman Arena where his hot dogs and hamburgers drew the fans as much as baseball or hockey.

The Denman Arena opened in 1911 at the corner of Georgia and Denman streets. With 10,500 seats, it was the biggest building of its kind in Canada until the Montreal Forum opened 15 years later. Inside the venue that hosted everything from hockey to wrestling to bicycle racing, Nat could be found behind the walk-up counter of his concession working the drink dispensers and the griddle. The fans might have come to see the Millionaires play hockey, but no one left without spending a dime at Nat's.

But he nearly lost it all on the night of August 19, 1936, when the Denman Arena went up in flames. "We raced down to the arena around 4 A.M.," recalled employee Bob Stout. "It went up like a tinder-box. By the time we arrived just the girders were standing." Nat's concession stand, one of his major sources of revenue, may have been reduced to ashes, but he carried right on.

For a time he continued to sell refreshments at Athletic Park. In the spring of 1944, the stadium was bought by Capilano Brewery interests. Six years and several fires later, the aging facility was finally torn down and replaced by Capilano Stadium at 30th Ave. and Ontario St. Today it is affectionately known as Nat Bailey Stadium, a paradise for fans who cherish baseball in the old-fashioned way: outside, with the sound of a base hit in the ear, a hot dog in one hand and a drink in the other. Nat's spirit truly lives on in the park named after Vancouver's "Mr. Baseball."

• Play ball! Athletic Park in the summer of '24: Collingwood vs. Young Liberals (Vancouver Senior Amateur Baseball League).

"freshly roasted" nuts – bagged earlier in the day and kept warm under the stands by a single electric bulb.

At the same time, he made a name for himself as "Caruso Nat," calling out batters' names in his musical tenor from the bleachers high above the diamond. All the while he continued to lob bags of peanuts to his customers, and they swore he never once missed catching the nickel tossed back in payment. Sadly, Nat's career as a sports announcer was cut short by a severe case of laryngitis. But his love of the crowd carried on.

He transformed his 1918 Model T truck into a travelling lunch-counter and parked it each Sunday at the ever-popular Lookout Point on SW Marine Dr. where hungry sightseers crowded around Nat's truck. They paid a dime for a hot dog, a nickel for an ice cream, then packed their families back into their cars and continued the weekend's drive. And it was there, in the woodlands south of Vancouver, that Nat found his inspiration for Canada's first drive-in on a hot summer day in 1924. Obviously too tired to contemplate the short walk to Nat's truck, one customer at the Point leaned out his car window and shouted, "Why don't you bring it to us?" By the next day Nat had hired three energetic young "hustlers" to take orders from the parked cars. Because they "hopped to it," they became known as carhops. For every sale they made, Nat paid them a penny commission.

In four years, Nat had turned that driver's casual call for service into the heart of a true family business. On a Saturday in June of 1928, he happily welcomed his guests to the first White Spot drive-in on Granville St. at 67th Ave. Friends and business acquaintances had scoffed at his gamble. In those days, the Marpole location wasn't even inside Vancouver city limits, but Nat had forged ahead, convinced that Granville St. would soon develop into a direct route to the United States; it was already on the Sunday loop out to Lookout Point.

As Nat stood there and watched the cars arrive, he must have thought that his friends had been right to be cautious, but surely he'd been right to be daring. Even little things were a trial the first time out. Levelling the lot, for instance. Years later Nat smiled at the thought. "The cost of clearing the lot was $11. I gave the workman a cheque for the amount. The bank honoured it, but notified me I was $7 overdrawn." He must have chuckled at his audacity, for

Nat's Hustlers

high in the stands of the Denman Arena, Roland "Rolly" McGee scanned the cheering crowd, hoping for a nod, a wave or a shout for a bag of peanuts or a cool soft drink. He was 14 years old, and Nat Bailey had taken him on as one of his employees. It was the dead centre of the Depression and Rolly wanted to impress his new boss. If Nat liked you, and you worked hard, there was good money to be made, money that kept a family going in tough times.

There were some good times too for a young man who enjoyed sports as much as Nat. "I remember one of the big events was a six-day bicycle race," recalled Rolly. "Teams of two came from all over the world to race non-stop, alternating sleeping and riding, with a 15-piece orchestra jazzing it up in the centre of the oval. It was a big job for us, selling peanuts, popcorn, hot dogs, hot drinks, ice cream, but we could make $8 to $10 a night, big money in those days. We took it home and gave most of it to our parents."

• "Hustler" Rolly McGee with his sisters Lorraine, left, and Helene, centre.

Dozens of young men worked with Nat and the White Spot family over the years and the experience left an indelible impression. In the words of Rolly McGee, "Nat Bailey was one of the fairest people. He treated you well as long as you worked hard, and he paid the highest of all the concession operators. He didn't hire a boy to sell, he hired a hustler. 'Get out there and hustle,'" he used to say.

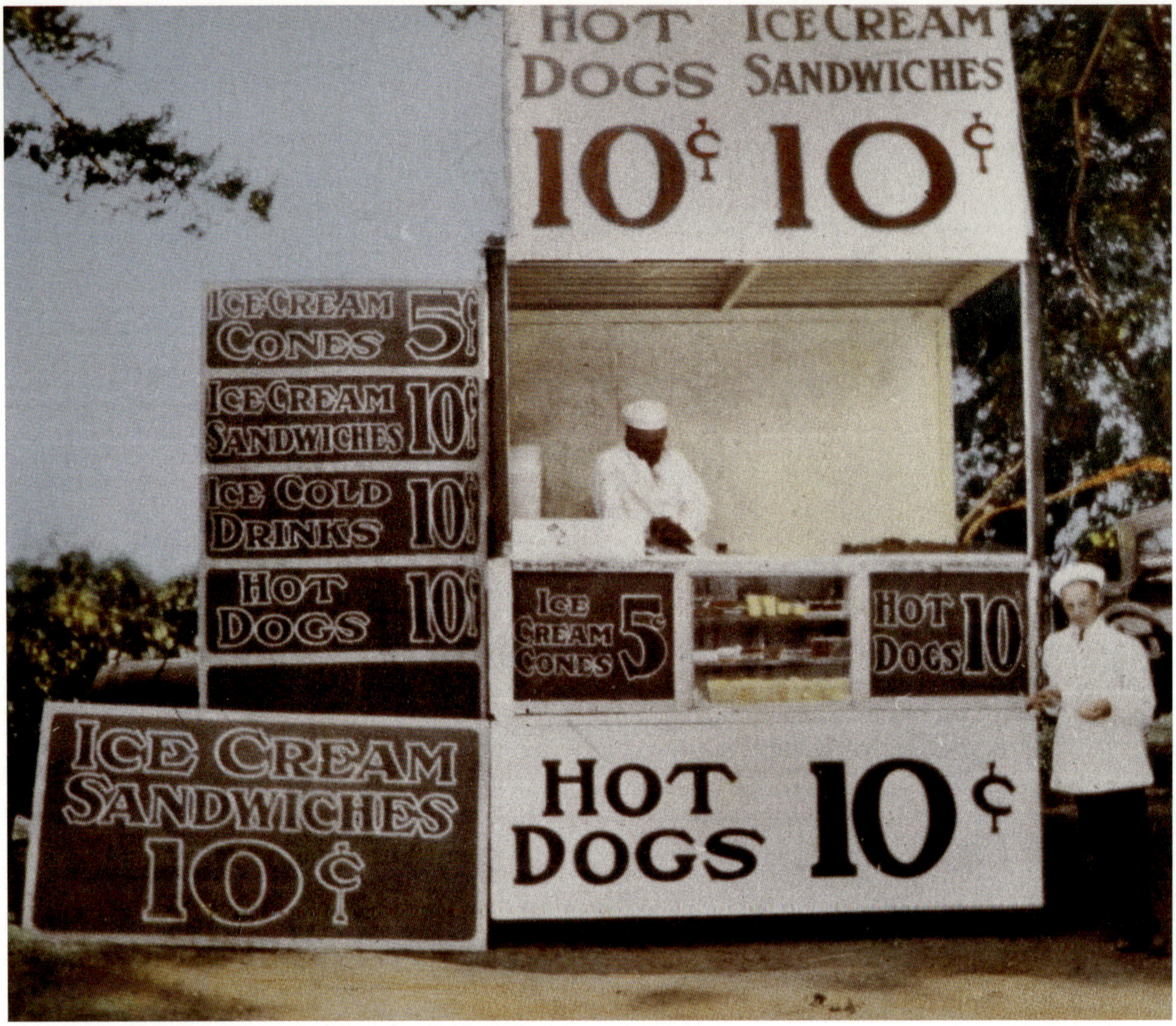

COURTESY OF GEORGE MITTLESTEAD

• Nat Bailey converted his Model T truck into a travelling lunch counter and parked at Lookout Point during the early 1920s. *Below left:* Nat's hustlers became carhops at Lookout Point serving 10¢ hot dogs and ice cream sandwiches. *Below right:* By 1925, Vancouver families on their Sunday drives regularly stopped to enjoy Nat's ice cream treats.

COURTESY OF GEORGE MITTLESTEAD

VANCOUVER PUBLIC LIBRARY 8021

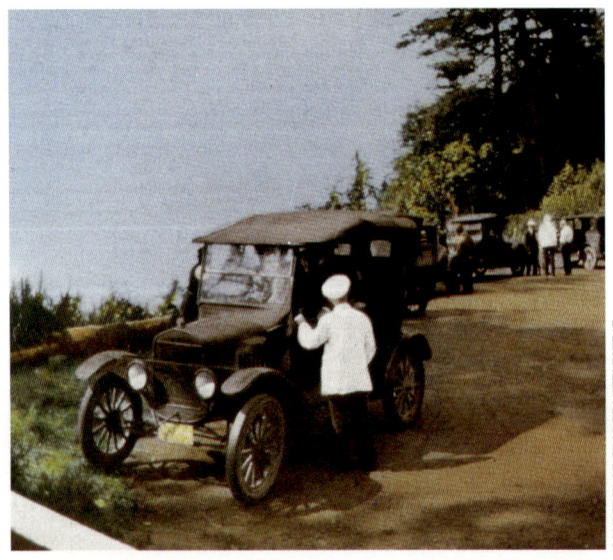

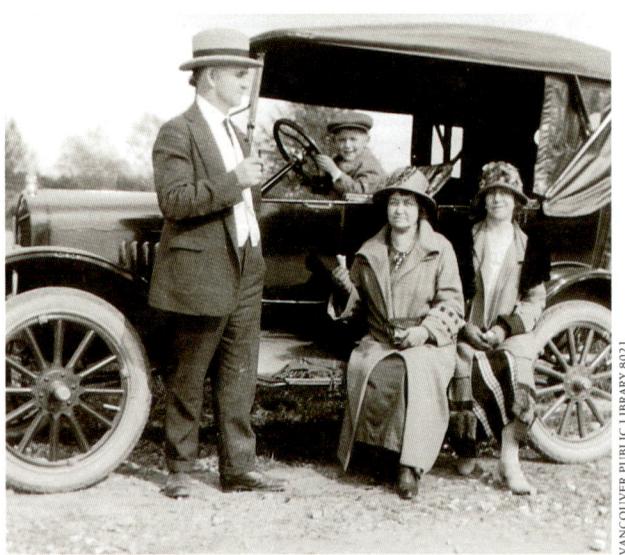

the drive-in itself, a landmark imitation log cabin, had cost $1,400 – far from peanuts in those days.

Behind Nat on the log cabin were two words in green: White Spot. His first idea for a name had been Granville Barbecue, but instead he took the advice of his friend, the late sportsman George Irwin. "Why not call it White Spot like that fellow on Wilshire Boulevard in Los Angeles?" he'd suggested. "He's doing all right with the name." So White Spot Barbecue it was, and Nat prayed that success would flow north.

Outside, cars jockeyed for space, while inside the log cabin, a joint of beef roasted on a spit in a big brick fireplace. "It was a real selling feature," says Helen Fawcett, an early White Spot customer, "because you could see the rotating meat through the window." But how to get delicious food from the kitchen to the 25 cars neatly parked in the drive-in and serve them all with a staff of two – only a cook and a manager who doubled as a carhop? Nat solved the problem with style by inventing the first carhop tray, using long one-half-inch by six-inch cedar planks painted white. Burgers, pop, coffee, almost anything could be balanced on it. So, like an elegant carnival performer, a carhop could slide hot food through the open windows of a car and magically turn it into a dining room on wheels. There was no tray like it anywhere in North America.

Not long after opening the White Spot Barbecue, Nat met Eva Ouelette, a waitress at Purdy's Restaurant on Granville St. She was a west coaster from a large Gabriola Island family, and through her Nat found the brothers and sisters he'd never had, while in her he discovered a lifelong partner who shared his dream of a true family restaurant business. For during the Depression, Eva took command of the White Spot Barbecue – known as the Drive-in by customers and employees alike – while Nat kept business humming at the ball park and beach concessions.

With one success behind him, Eva's support and a bit of the gambler in his blood, Nat was ready to take another chance. In 1930, at the age of 28, he opened a second White Spot Barbecue at Slocan and Hastings streets, a replica of the original, to serve the driving public crossing the Second Narrows Bridge. But if the wheel of fortune can grant delight, it can also serve up disaster. Almost as soon as the new

The Original Drive-in

The roads were often little better than dirt tracks, which is exactly what made driving in the late 1920s in Vancouver so exciting. People went for long drives, often out to rustic autocamps in Burnaby and the Fraser Valley. For an afternoon treat, young people would pile into a friend's automobile and set out for a "Sunday drive," and if they drove out Granville St. to Marine Dr., White Spot was the perfect place to stop for a bite.

When Nat Bailey launched Canada's first drive-in restaurant in 1928, the trend toward car ownership was taking off. Between 1920 and 1929 the number of cars in the Lower Mainland shot up from 6,500 to 36,500.

Even during the Depression, the parking lot at Granville and 67th often overflowed – because a burger at "The Spot" on a cool summer night was made to order and the customers came in waves. The evening shift would start at 7 P.M., and the rush flowed steadily between 9 P.M. and 10 P.M. when the movies ended on Granville's Theatre Row. After 11 P.M., the beer parlour crowd cruised in, respectfully obeying the house rule of "no fights or you're out."

And the White Spot staff were often there until the last car or revellers wandered home – even if the sun was rising when the carhops finally got to bed.

• Relaxing afternoon at the Restmore Lodge Auto Park.

• *Top:* White Spot #1 drive-in lot in 1931. *Above:* Nat, second from left, and carhops celebrate during construction in 1928. *Left:* Eva, fourth from right, and waitresses in the late 1940s.

• *Top:* The original White Spot Barbecue opened in June, 1928 at Granville St. and 67th Ave. *Centre left:* Eddie Gorman (right) and friend hit "The Spot," 1932. *Left:* That same year Nat remodelled his creation. *Above:* Jack Monahan's friend poses beside his car featuring a White Spot promotional wheel cover.

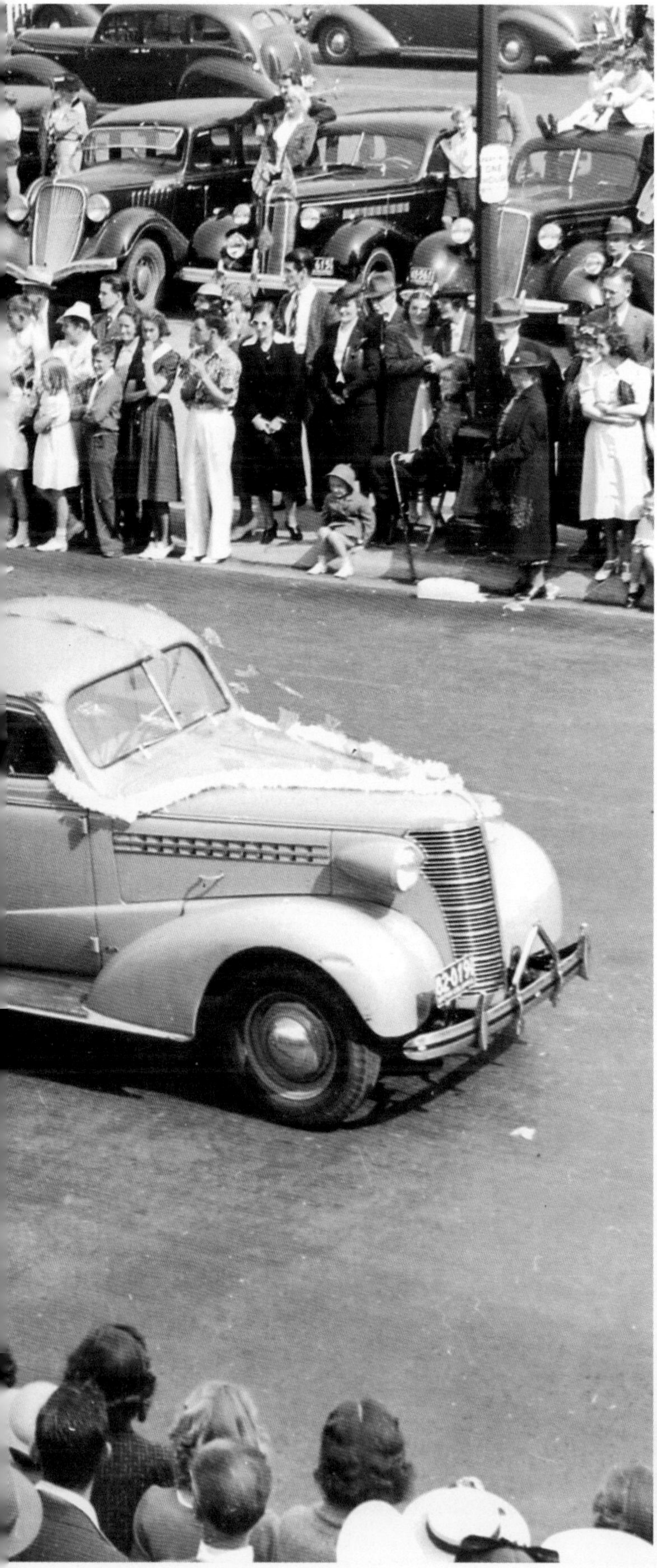

White Spot opened, a freighter wedged itself under the bridge, and ripped it apart with the rising tide. Without the bridge open, automobile traffic slowed to a trickle, and the parking lot sat nearly empty day after day. White Spot #2 failed, and Nat nearly lost his shirt in the process.

Hard economic times took their toll on the business. "White Spot #1 teetered on the brink for some years. Only the loyal help of his wife and the earnings of his mobile truck kept the venture solvent," observed Hal Smallman in a 1961 article in *Canadian Food Journal.* Yet people tend to manufacture their own good luck, so to make ends meet Nat worked the airshows at the old Vancouver Airport, in addition to his concessions at Athletic Park and Denman Arena. He used radio ads to attract customers and sent "the boys" (as his male staff were called) to Granville Street's Theatre Row to place flyers on the windshields of parked cars. Nat and Eva refused to give in to the hard times, and with their dedicated family of staff, they got their beloved White Spot through those lean years.

By the mid-1930s, the future began to brighten. Eva took over the management of the Lunch Room (renamed Marine Spot in 1937) in the $2.5-million Marine Building, a beautiful Art Deco structure which seemed to embody the hope and desire that fuelled many people in the Depression. And in that spirit Nat purchased property adjacent to his original lot. Soon he was ready to build on it. In 1937, the White Spot Restaurant and Drive-in replaced the original log cabin barbecue as White Spot #1. Uncharacteristically for Nat, the Baileys' new restaurant opened with very little fanfare because they had something even bigger in the works – perhaps the biggest gamble of Nat's entire career. That gamble would be the White Spot Dining Room. •

VANCOUVER PUBLIC LIBRARY 11646, *RIGHT:* STUART THOMSON PHOTO, CITY OF VANCOUVER ARCHIVES, CVA 99-4469

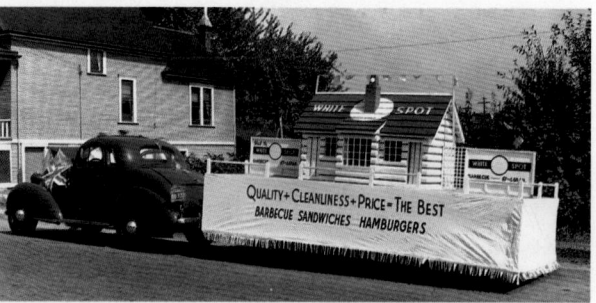

• *Left:* In 1938 White Spot celebrated its first decade of success and service with a float in the PNE parade. *Above:* An earlier White Spot float from the 1936 PNE parade.

Staying Power

The White Spot started small, as families most often do. And like most families that grow to be large, there's a clutch of happy rogues at the core of it.

Nat began with two partners, Cecil "Cec" Eustace and Jack Monahan. Cec was one of Nat's original carhops at the Lookout in south Vancouver while Jack was manager of the Barbecue before opening his own diner in late 1930. Other longtime employees joined in the 1930s: Bob Stout, Art Jones, Ernie Creamer, and Roy "Parky" Parkinson. Together with Cec, they made up the five partners who would work shoulder-to-shoulder with "Mr. B," as they called him, building White Spot's future.

Bob joined the company in 1934 as a carhop and his career with the family would span six decades. When Art first started at White Spot in 1936 he was carhopping to pay his university tuition and would eventually manage all the drive-ins. Ernie, appropriately enough, began as a fountain boy preparing milkshakes and sundaes, and would go on to be the manager of Ernie's Fine Foods, White Spot's Kentucky Fried Chicken franchise for B.C. Finally, Parky joined White Spot in 1938, working part-time at the Drive-in. After World War II, he climbed up the ranks from fleet driver to partner within nine years. In 1961, he opened the historic Victoria White Spot, the first outside the Lower Mainland, staying on until his retirement in 1969.

Of course, women also play a central role in most big happy families, and Eva Bailey was the soul of this one. Her knowledge of fine dining transformed White Spot. While Nat and his partners contemplated new locations, she went about cementing the company's reputation for honesty and quality. She attended to every detail in the Dining Room, even contributing recipes – including her mother's plum pudding which became a customer favourite. Later she was joined by her sister Millie Kelly and three nieces.

But this particular family had a wide embrace. Eva and Nat saw to it that all of their employees enjoyed security, an opportunity for advancement and good wages. Moreover, in successful families there is always an inheritance. Eva and Nat's strong values have endured to this day, and ensure that the current White Spot is still an employee's home away from home.

• *Left:* Cecil Eustace (left) and Doug Morrison were carhops in 1940. *Centre:* Jack Monahan and giant postcard, a late 1920s White Spot mural. *Right:* Three men of the kitchen: Jack Boyle, John Stark and Bob Stout, late 1930s.

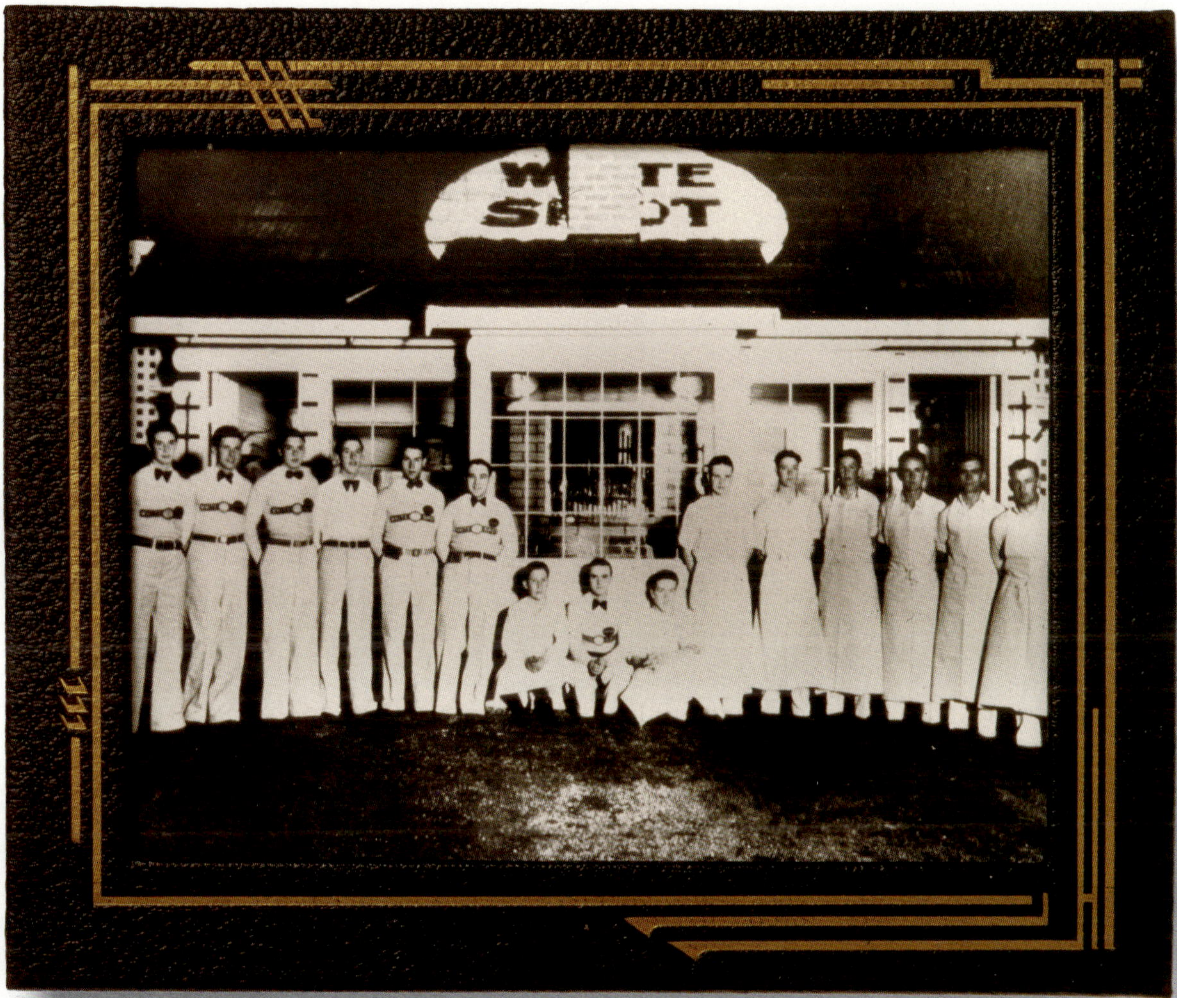

COURTESY OF WILF TRICE

• *Above:* Nat (far right) with original Barbecue staff, 1929. *Below:* Dining Room waitresses with Nat after the 1938 opening.

COURTESY OF R.J. STOUT

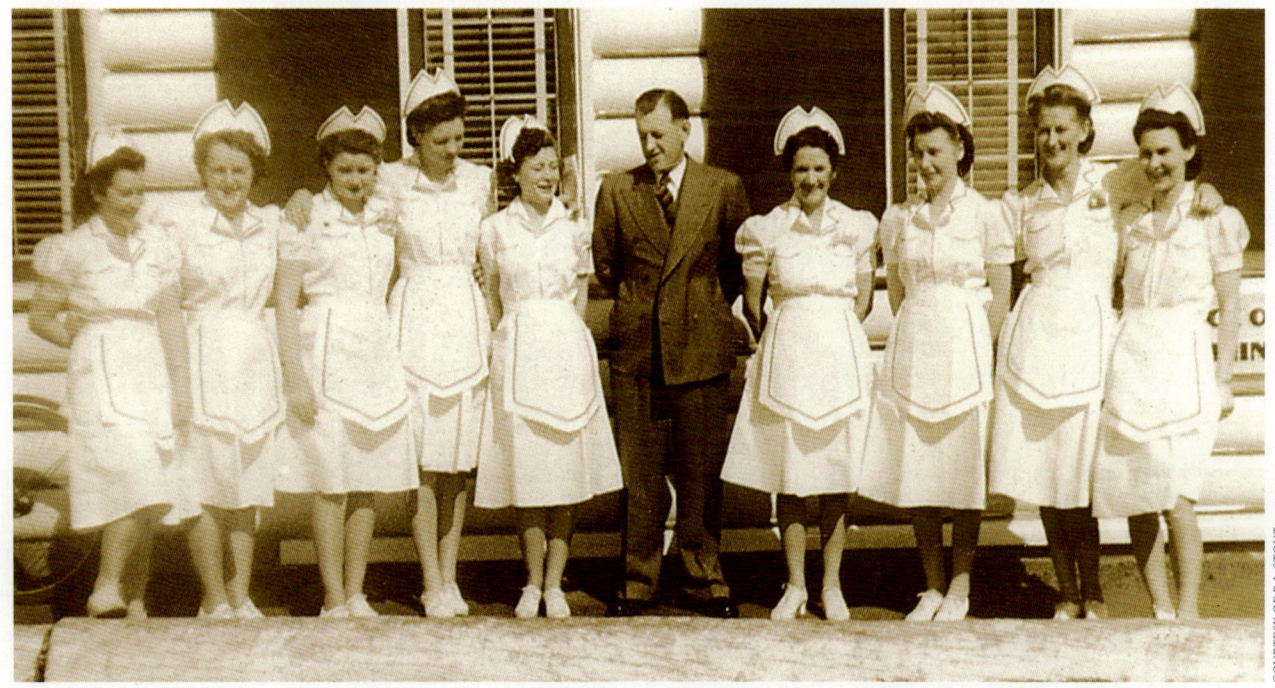

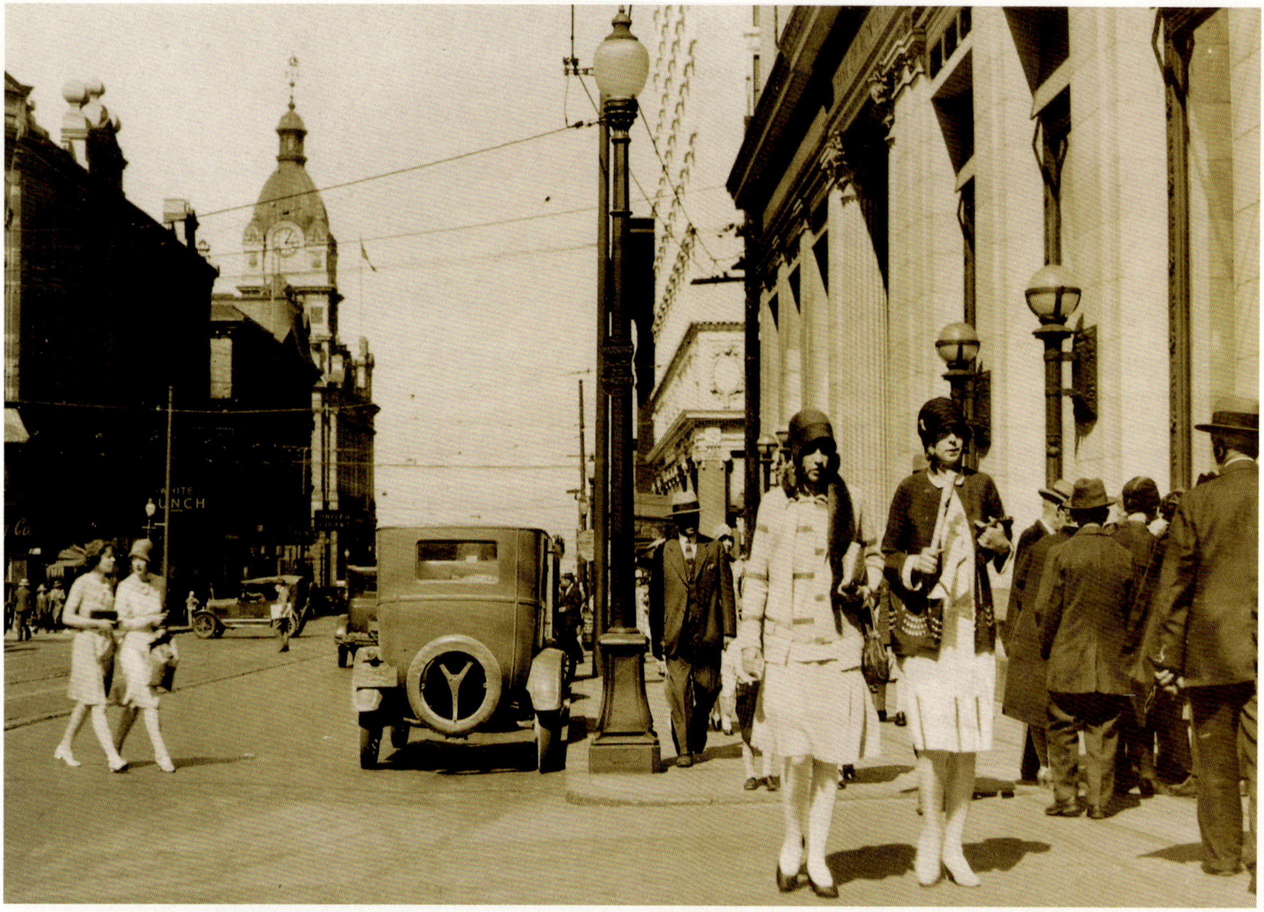

VANCOUVER PUBLIC LIBRARY 7753

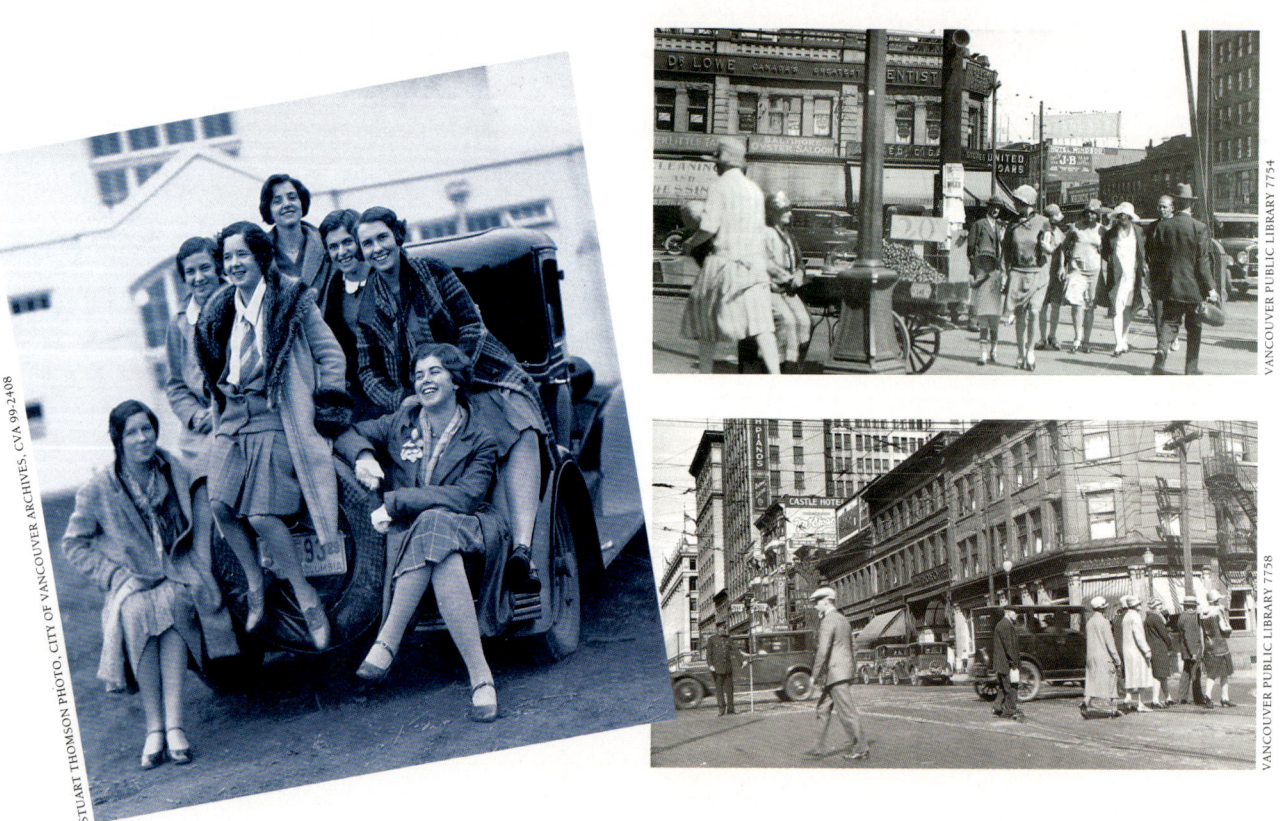

• It's 1928 and Vancouver is booming. *Above:* The fashions of Granville Street near Pender. *Centre right:* The bustle of Hastings and Carrall. *Bottom:* The hum of Granville and Robson. *Left:* Society girls on the move.

STUART THOMSON PHOTO, CITY OF VANCOUVER ARCHIVES, CVA 99-2408

VANCOUVER PUBLIC LIBRARY 7754

VANCOUVER PUBLIC LIBRARY 7758

A Roller-Coaster Era

• The year of the White Spot, 1928, brought forth another champion. Vancouver's Percy Williams (left) won Olympic gold for Canada.

White Spot's first decade was a roller-coaster era. From the heyday of the Roaring Twenties to the depths of the Great Depression, from flappers in headbands and short skirts to unemployed workers on the breadlines, the years from 1928 to 1938 were challenging ones for Canadians. In 1928, the year hometown sprinter Percy Williams captured two Olympic gold medals, an evening at the Pantages vaudeville theatre cost 50¢ a ticket and the factory price for a Chevrolet roadster was $665. By 1932, with 650,000 unemployed men in Canada, many of them in Vancouver, even such simple pleasures were out of reach. It was a long slow climb out of the Depression but by 1936, the city's 50th birthday, optimistic crowds lined the parade routes. By the time King George IV and Queen Elizabeth toured the streets of Vancouver to cheering crowds in 1939, World War II was on the horizon. Another new era was beginning. Difficult though it was, it was also the start of renewed prosperity.

• Bird's-eye view of the royal couple during their Vancouver tour in 1939.

1938-1949 The Expansion Years

Nat Bailey's instinct and acumen formed a large part of his success during the White Spot expansion years. But above all, it was his love of people that motivated him and opened doors. By the late 1930s everyone in Vancouver recognized Nat. Wearing his trademark bow-tie, he'd trade shop talk with his suppliers or drop in at the local garage for gas and gossip. Checking on sales at White Spot #1, Nat would stroll by the parked cars and share a word or two with his guests. And what they told him he paid attention to: they were tired of the Depression; they wanted to dress up and get away from it all. But, with the exception of the fancy dining room at the Hotel Vancouver, there was no place to go.

The man with the bow-tie nodded his appreciation and went away to set the wheels in motion for a new White Spot concept which would combine three restaurant styles on the same site at Granville and 67th. Little by little, he bought up the property adjacent to the original White Spot Barbecue. Nat and Eva put their plan together, and in 1937, he replaced the Barbecue with the White Spot Restaurant and Drive-in. The following year the White Spot Dining Room was added. Nat's vision seemed complete.

The Baileys opened the Dining Room's doors on a memorable Saturday night in 1938. To a public clamouring for good times and good food it was nothing short of a miracle: a sophisticated, ultra-modern, affordable destination for lunch or dinner. Elegant couples in dinner dress sat in their cars for hours waiting for a table. Heralded in the press and on radio, the Dining Room was an overnight sensation, and for many years it would rival the popularity of the best restaurants in Vancouver.

To Nat Bailey it was a coming of age. He and Eva personally greeted guests by name at the door. On many a night, a celebrity or two would dine there, an anniversary party would be in full swing, or a young couple would shyly enjoy their first date.

Yet as much as the Baileys opened their doors to the community, they treated their restaurant as a home. To Nat and Eva their staff were family, and most of them were neighbours as well. Trained with care by Eva, White Spot waitresses, carhops and kitchen staff were usually local residents. Peggy Parkinson, who started in the Dining Room at the age of 17, called them the Marpole Kids. "Whole families from the Marpole area would come to work at the Spot. As many as nine Miller

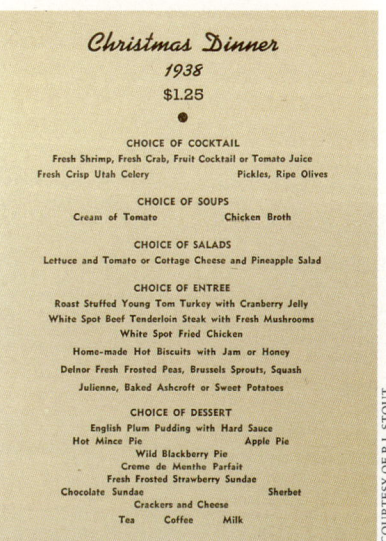

• White Spot Christmas dinner menu, 1938. *Facing page:* The smiles of service and satisfaction: Nat Bailey and Dining Room server Margaret Miller.

• *Above:* The spirit of Christmas glows in the warmth of the Dining Room, 1938. *Below:* The Drive-in bustles in the 1940s.

kids worked there over time, as well as six Peters, four Goddards and members of a dozen other families. It was a real family deal."

It was not only the Dining Room that proved a success. Next door, the restaurant did a roaring business. As a young man, Rolly McGee worked for Nat. "It was the first classy drive-in we had in Vancouver," he says. "It had a white rail fence and a beautiful Cape Cod style building painted white and green. 'Let's go to the White Spot,' you used to say if you wanted to impress somebody."

If Nat Bailey had built the new Dining Room in response to his customers' desire to escape the realities of the Depression, he surely hadn't foreseen that a global conflict would propel his adopted city and country into the next decade. Ernie Creamer recalled a busy Sunday when the staff had just closed the doors and he was taking a break with the kitchen staff. Over the radio came the sobering news: Canada had entered World War II. "It was a very solemn atmosphere," he recollected.

Like his employees, Nat Bailey was now unsure of the future. But he was certain of the present and of the people who had helped him to make it a successful one. He promised his employees who enlisted that their jobs would be there for them when they returned, and many of them – women and men, staff and management – went off to war. Nat and Eva were proud to see them go, but they were left struggling to fill the gaps in their White Spot family as well as maintain the high quality of food as rationing took its toll.

During the war, girl hops replaced enlisted men at the Drive-in, while serving staff peeled and chipped their own potatoes. Rationing restricted the use of butter, sugar, meat, tea, coffee and liquor. These limitations, combined with the requirement that no meat was to be served on Tuesdays and Fridays, led to a refinement of the White Spot menu. Chicken, cheese and fish dishes appeared. Not surprisingly, fish 'n' chips was a popular item, and so was the foot-long White Spot hot dog. Both were overnight successes. Yet despite these innovations and the loyalty of his clients, Nat feared that the operation would die because of gas and tire rationing. "He thought the drive-in business would go down the

• **The corner of Granville and 67th was known simply as "The Spot" –** *the* **place to be.**

The Most Talked-about Room in Town

In 1938 the opening of the White Spot Dining Room created a splash. Although Canada was still recovering from the Depression, the Baileys went all out to create a restaurant worthy of the hopes people were beginning to feel about the future.

The Dining Room featured Vancouver's first knotty pine interior and started a city-wide trend for recreation rooms in that style. A giant fireplace cast a soft glow over the room, the warmth enhanced by an advanced "heatilator" unit. Cozy booths lined the walls, while in the centre of the room guests sat at custom-made maple tables.

While Nat ran the concessions, Eva was the force behind the Dining Room. She trained the staff to serve in the sophisticated atmosphere of linen tablecloths, fine silverware, and finger bowls. At first only waitresses served in the Dining Room. However, since the place was heated by the big fireplace, strong arms were required to bring in four foot alder logs, so waiters were hired. As Ernie Creamer recalled, "We wore white uniforms with little black patent leather bow-ties. The tips were better in the Dining Room!"

Above all, the food kept guests returning. Prepared in the city's first stainless steel kitchen, the menu was mouth-watering: chicken fried in a deep skillet and eight-ounce tenderloin steaks served with hearty helpings of potatoes and "frosted" green peas. Baking powder biscuits and greengage plum jam came with every meal. For dessert Eva offered freshly baked fruit pie à la mode, and at the end of the meal she would come to the table bearing coffees with thick whipped cream.

On opening night cars crowded the lot, couples lined up to get in, and Eva and Nat greeted their guests at the door to a room like no other in Vancouver. Dinner at home was simply dinner. At the Baileys' it was truly dining out.

- *Below:* The Dining Room was in its heyday in 1942 despite the pressures of the war.
Right: Group portrait of Dining Room servers in the 1940s.

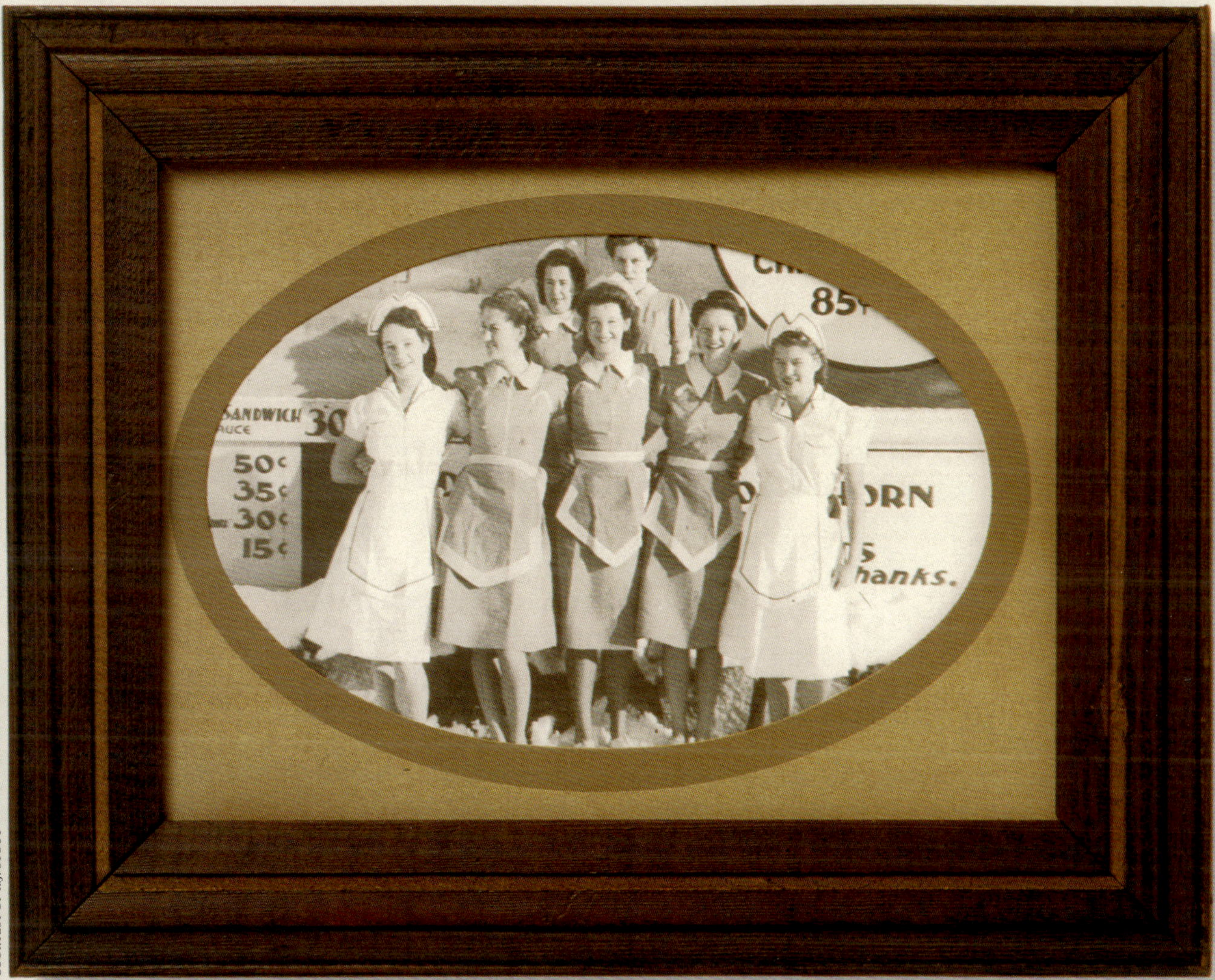

COURTESY OF R.J. STOUT

COURTESY OF MARK AND RYAN ANDREWS

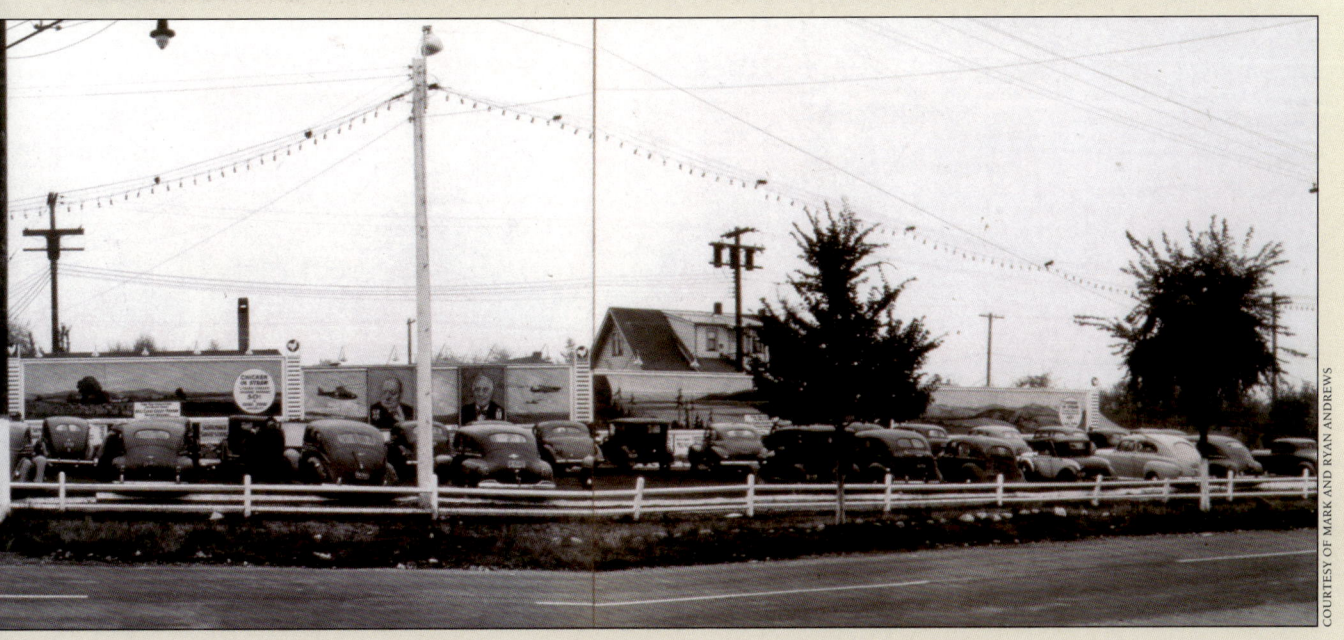

• *Above:* This 1945 Dining Room placemat, like the famous murals, mimicked the style of postcards and became another White Spot instant classic.

WHITE SPOT

Building an ever increasing patronage on . . .

Quality Food -- Cleanliness and Pleasing Service

★

Left: Scene showing present day dinner hour - - JUNE 1945.

Below: The original White Spot - - JUNE 1928.

COURTESY OF GEORGE MITTLESTEAD

Whistling up to "The Spot"

mildred Wylie's first memories of White Spot go back to 1930 when she was 13 years old. Tucked into a two seat roadster, she and her 20-year-old stepsister whistled up to White Spot #1. "As a teenager, going to the White Spot was a special treat. Of course they had places like that in California but, except for White Spot, we didn't have them up here."

After graduating from Kitsilano High School, Millie left for nursing college in Victoria where she met her husband-to-be David Wylie. Back in Vancouver, the young couple often drove to White Spot in Millie's new Ford Model A.

"Dave and I both worked shifts. Every chance we got we'd catch the afternoon concerts in Stanley Park. After that, we went to live it up at White Spot. The food was excellent; Dave loved the chiffon pineapple pie that was three inches high."

After the war, going to White Spot became a family affair for the Wylies and their two children. "Other White Spots opened up . . . when the kids were older, we took them to Cambie and King Edward on special occasions, like when everyone passed their exams."

At 76 Millie still likes to whistle up to a few of her favourite White Spots. She smiles at the thought: "White Spot fits in tremendously with Vancouver life."

- **White Spot was always a part of the Wylie family life: David, Paul and Millie, 1947**

COURTESY OF MILLIE WYLIE

tube," Ernie Creamer said, "but it didn't happen. People seemed to have enough gas and we flourished." In fact, by the war's end, White Spot had won an uncontested place in the hearts of Vancouverites. As longtime Dining Room hostess Della Sturby recalled, the Baileys' guests were treated like members of the family. At Christmas, regular customers would give gifts to the senior staff or leave a holiday bonus instead of the usual tip. In fact, before the advent of country clubs many of the city's prominent families would ask Della and her staff to organize special parties for them, and it was common for the staff to arrange the room for festive occasions such as a birthday gathering or a wedding shower.

With the end of the war came a resurgence of confidence all across the land. By now well established on his original site in south Vancouver, Nat too yearned for new opportunities. As usual, he was quick off the mark. In 1945 Nat established Newton Farms in Surrey, B.C. to cultivate the high quality and vast quantity of chicken and fresh produce that White Spot needed. Then in 1946 he built a small replica of the Barbecue on the southeast corner of the property to handle the weekend and holiday overflow. And in 1947 the replica was moved to Kingsway and Gladstone St. where an addition was later built and operated by Roy Parkinson, one of Nat's future partners.

White Spot also continued to run various concessions, such as the teahouse adjacent to the Cliffhouse Dining Room at Whytecliff in West Vancouver, which it managed for one magical summer in 1947. The restaurant was idyllic, built on stilts overlooking Howe Sound and the Bowen Island ferries that

Tray Deluxe

drive-ins flourish due to motor cars, so it's no surprise that Nat Bailey indulged in a little custom automotive design. He created long wooden trays that carhops slid across the open windows of a car.

The trays worked perfectly on a sunny day, but Vancouver has a hundred kinds of rain to offer its guests. Nat manufactured a second version which would prevent runoff, made from shorter lengths of wood with expandable hardware so the tray could be attached to the inside door sill. Now the car windows could be closed and Triple-O sauce would not be diluted by drizzle.

However, the original wooden trays needed frequent repairs and painting. Stainless steel was experimented with next, but it was too heavy. In 1948, Nat commissioned a local company to produce a lighter, less cumbersome aluminum model.

• Carhop Brent Simon demonstrates a unique adaptation of the White Spot tray in the 1970s.

For many years there was no tray like it anywhere, and it was highlighted in industry magazines. With every publication, White Spot received inquiries from other restaurants in moist climates. But dry food sometimes commands a high price, and at $25 a tray, Nat didn't have many takers.

Like all good inventions, perfection takes time, and these trays still sported one problem – aluminum oxide, a hand-blackening substance that was the bane of a carhop's existence. Finally in the 1960s, White Spot created a new moulded fibreglass model that is still in use today, rain or shine, at the remaining 16 drive-ins and 2 drive-throughs. There, these telescoping trays can be seen propped across two motorcycles, balanced between lawn chairs or even extended lengthwise (from dashboard to trunk) in sports cars.

Only in a city like Vancouver could rain be the mother of invention!

docked there. Peggy Parkinson remembers that "people would drive up, their cars filled with kids, and ferry over to Bowen. For the White Spot staff who worked in the teahouse, it was like a summer holiday."

But for Nat, holidays were few and far between. Always on the go, puffing his way through three packs of cigarettes a day, he read westerns in his spare time instead of going for picnics on nearby islands. And when he wasn't indulging his passion for Zane Grey, he was opening new restaurants, one at Georgia and Burrard streets between the Ritz Hotel and the Palomar Supper Club. As if to make up for the low key opening of the Restaurant and Drive-in 11 years earlier, Nat launched this new operation with a splash: a helicopter settled on the parking lot and a stewardess emerged to serve the first customers. Once again, White Spot was the place to see and be seen in. In fact, in Marpole the name was borrowed by at least three others: Ivor Pott's White Spot Barber Shop (later the home of White Spot Hardware), Sid Morrey's White Spot Service Station, and the White Spot Grocery. The Baileys welcomed the flattery. "It didn't bother Nat they were using the name," says Bob Stout. "They were all good neighbours."

At the centre of it all were Nat and Eva, he the renowned local sportsman, entrepreneur, community friend, she the soul of the Dining Room, the heart of the White Spot family. For 20 years they had worked together and around them were the fruits of that labour: a business that seemed more family than mere profits and loss, and a reputation for warmth, consideration and excellence. It was based on this success that the White Spot legend flourished into the second half of the century. •

• **Throughout the '50s White Spot aluminum service trays lightened the loads of carhops used to the heavier wooden originals.**

War-time Girl Hops

"Save The Empire" was the call to arms in 1939 and most White Spot carhops responded to it.

Nat and Eva now turned to women as part of a trend which saw females in all areas of the labour force double from 30,000 to 60,000 in the first four years of the new decade.

The first White Spot "girl hops," including Eileen Barker and Ann Miller, came on board in 1941. In 1943, waitress Peggy Parkinson donned white trousers and joined them. "There were only Cec (Eustace) and two girl hops during the week, so I worked in the Dining Room until 9 P.M., then at the Drive-in till midnight," she recalled. "We were run off our feet on Friday and Saturday until 2 A.M. serving families, servicemen and piles of teenagers who were dating."

The war took its toll on White Spot staff. Bill Poritt and brothers Tom and Bruce Kirkham, all with the RCAF, were killed in Europe. The Kirkham boys died on the same day in the same air raid.

Before the war, Nat had promised his staff that their jobs would be awaiting them when they returned, and he was true to his word. When the men returned they traded in their khakis for a carhop's uniform. The girl hops moved on to other White Spot positions or like so many women at the time, they took the call for peace to heart and left the White Spot family to begin ones of their own.

• Girl hops were the mainstay of White Spot's success during the war years.

COURTESY OF R.J. STOUT

• Vancouver delivers the goods! Vancouverites bought victory bonds, then in 1945 celebrated the triumph they had helped secure.

• *Inset left:* In 1947 White Spot took over management of the Cliffhouse at Whytecliff Park. *Above:* Peggy Parkinson, Nat and Eva at Whytecliff. *Inset right:* A White Spot picnic for enlisted staff home on leave.

• The 1940 White Spot fishing derby. *Left to right:* John Milne, Roy Parkinson, Eileen Barker, Ernie Creamer, George Moore, unidentified guest, Willa Borhaven, Bill Nichol.

Better than Homemade

from the start, White Spot fare had to be absolutely fresh, nothing frozen or processed, a tradition that largely remains to this day.

During World War II, however, it took creativity to keep up the standards. As White Spot's informal historian Bob Stout recollected, "Nat had a hell of a time during the war years. There was rationing and it was tough to get the necessary staples. If you were a credit customer, you were entitled to a certain amount of goods, but because Nat paid cash he had to do a little bit of black market work on the side."

By the mid-1940s, Nat had come up with a unique solution to his supply problems. He bought property in Surrey, B.C. and started Newton Farms, to provide chickens and fresh produce to White Spot restaurants. New approaches worked in the Commissary, as well, where staff prepared White Spot's menu items. Giant refrigerators contained perishables and huge sides of beef and a new-fangled hamburger machine turned out up to 1,800 patties an hour.

Some time after he opened his third location, Nat got into the habit of driving around to each one in turn, ordering hamburgers with Triple-O sauce to ensure that his product tasted the same wherever a customer went. Occasionally he tried to disguise his identity from a new carhop – usually without success. "Coming right up, Mr. Bailey," the new employee would chirrup, spoiling the founder's cat-and-mouse adventure.

• White Spot came to Vancouver's heart at Georgia and Burrard in 1948. In addition to drive-in service, it offered breakfast for the first time. A helicopter landing was the highlight of the opening day festivities.

A Legend of its Own

Indubitably, the best known of all White Spot menu items is its Legendary Hamburger. What makes it doubly famous is Triple-O sauce, an addictive combination of White Spot's own secret ingredients.

Legend has it that the name was part of the shorthand language of the carhops: guests could choose from mayonnaise and relish, and the order slips were printed with three X's and three O's. An X meant hold, an O meant extra and Triple-O meant plenty of everything.

While the precise origin of Triple-O sauce is a matter of speculation, there is no doubt about the powerful lure of the special sauce. White Spot burgers have been airfreighted across Canada and around the world. Indeed, many a returning traveller, like Vancouver writer Kerry McPhedran, has demanded to be taken straight to White Spot from the airport. "After three years in Europe, I ordered three burgers with Triple-O," she recalled gleefully.

Triple-O sauce has won the hearts of locals and visitors alike. As Denny Boyd wrote in a 1986 Vancouver Sun column, ". . . no 30-day ad campaign could ever conjure up anything as indelible as the Triple-O concept. . . . The White Spot to me means Triple-O's and Nat Bailey in a wash-and-wear shirt and a blue clip-on bow-tie. . . . White Spot is as indigenously Vancouver as the 9-o'clock gun. . ."

• PNE parade marches past the Georgia and Burrard location in 1949.

1949-1960 The Boom Years

Interviewed in his office above White Spot at Granville and 67th, Nat Bailey scoffed at the mention of hobbies. "Haven't any others," he told writer Louis Katin in the mid-1950s, gesturing around the sparsely outfitted room. "This is my only hobby – full-time and spare-time too."

White Spot had been Nat's life for more than two decades and everything he did was part of his formula for success. He gave unstintingly to the community, donating both time and money to a dozen groups, from the Marpole Rotary Club (of which he was a founder) and the local Chamber of Commerce to little league teams and a junior pipe band. His every action embodied White Spot's underlying philosophy. "Nat was fiercely loyal to you, as long as you gave him quality," said Jack Diamond, a Rotary associate and local businessman. White Spot staff also knew that Nat and Eva expected the best and offered the same in return. "To their credit, if they yelled at you, you were free to yell back," said partner Roy Parkinson. "They had high standards and if you could meet them, you felt proud to work for the company."

As yet, the 51-year-old founder of White Spot was showing no signs of slowing down, and that was a style that suited the postwar decade. Business boomed, new products hit the market and people finally had money to spend. Indeed, when staff and customers celebrated White Spot's 25th anniversary in 1953, growth was the byword, and two years later four new drive-ins and an additional dining room had opened. The statistics of the $1.5 million success may seem small by current standards, but it is still astonishing that a family business in 1955 Vancouver had 350 staff members who served 110,000 restaurant guests a week, while 10,000 cars a day wheeled into the drive-ins. Nat now had five partners, all longtime employees (Art Jones, Cecil Eustace, Ernie Creamer, Roy Parkinson and Bob Stout). Like a new generation, they ran the restaurants for him under their own employee group, with Nat owning the properties, and remaining as a president deeply involved in the details of the business and the group of people he loved.

• Promotional matchbooks were part of the SMILE! campaign in 1955. *Facing page: Georgia and Granville, Christmas 1957.*

These were banner times for White Spot. It was cited in the prestigious *Holiday* magazine as one of 72 eating places in North America recommended to travellers. "Sizzling steaks, chicken. Not too expensive," it recommended. They were good days, too, for Nat personally. The press nicknamed him the "Sultan of Sandwiches," a title he heartily approved. His office above the original site buzzed with activity and was a "mecca for a horde of friends," as a *Province* writer noted in a 1955 personality profile. There was always someone trying to grab a minute of Nat's time – generous to a fault, Nat rarely turned anyone away.

A couple of times a week, Nat drove to each White Spot location, his two grandsons and their pals in tow, checking on the quality of the food and the promptness of the service. "We were the luckiest kids in the world," said grandson Mark Andrews. "What other kids could have all the hamburgers and pop they could eat?" And while the grandchildren dined, Nat kibitzed with guests, or offered a word

They All Dined at White Spot

From the very start, the White Spot Dining Room at Granville and 67th was a popular stop for out-of-town celebrities. Jack Benny, Mary Livingstone, Dennis Day, Bing Crosby, Mary Martin, Xavier Cugat and Wayne and Shuster, to name a few, all dined there.

After 1952, the Georgia and Burrard White Spot, located beside the Palomar Supper Club and just up the street from the Hotel Vancouver, also attracted a lot of night people, particularly entertainers playing the Cave or the Palomar. Joy Metcalfe of CKNW and *The Courier* worked for *Celebrity Review* at the Cave during its last three years. She remembers escorting the likes of Henry Mancini, Robert Goulet and Van Johnson from the smoke and noise of the club to a source of fresh air and late night good food at the White Spot on Georgia. "Americans always loved hamburgers and they had heard about White Spot's reputation. They would order a hamburger because of the special Triple-O sauce."

There were many other familiar faces too – Frankie Laine, Juliet, Jack Teagarden, the Harlem Globetrotters and local notables Jack Cullen, Dal Richards, Claude Logan, Mart Kenny and His Western Gentlemen all welcomed many a dawn there. And Mel Torme would always head for the White Spot and clear the velvet fog with a hamburger.

• **A 1943 luncheon celebrating Nat and Eva's receipt of a victory banner for war bond sales. Jack Benny led the tribute and brought the cast of his show along. Left to right: Don Wilson, Jack, his wife Mary, Phil Harris, Vera Vague and Dennis Day (who went from this luncheon to join the U.S. Navy).**

of investment advice to friends.

For Nat, untiring dedication to his business was an enjoyable way of life. A founder of the Canadian Restaurant Association, six-time president of the Vancouver Restaurant Association and a member of the American Restaurant Association, Nat was frequently in demand as a speaker at conventions. These out-of-town trips, to exotic places like Mexico or New York City, doubled as holidays. After one such vacation, Eva Bailey complained to a friend, "We went 2,000 miles to visit 2,000 restaurants. You call that a holiday?" And if it wasn't restaurants, it was baseball games.

In fact, Nat became progressively more involved in his favourite sport, rarely missing a ball game at Capilano Stadium. By the late 1950s, he was a part owner of the Vancouver Mounties, a star-crossed triple-A team that demanded his energies until 1969 when the team finally folded. Typically, his passion for sports was reflected in his activities at White Spot. In the fall of 1954, for example, the restaurants ran a Grey Cup football forecast pool with 168 prizes of hamburgers and coffee given away to White Spot guests in the first week alone.

The 1950s was a decade of promotional innovation – it was perhaps best epitomized by the advent of the suburban mall and when the Park Royal Shopping Centre opened in West Vancouver in May 1955 it was the largest of its kind in Canada. White Spot launched the Park Royal Drive-in and Coffee Shop, which instantly became a hit. So tight was the opening schedule that the managers were painting bumper logs minutes before the first cars rolled in, and Sunday staff wrote up orders in the line-up of vehicles so meals were ready by the time customers had parked.

Things were moving at a fast and furious pace, and to keep track of the changes, White Spot employees (between 60 and 70 people) met weekly to share ideas and procedures. Always alert to new possibilities, Nat brought in experts on everything from the art of carhopping to the method of preparing set-ups. These brainstorming sessions may have been

• **Top:** Nat, the "Sultan of Sandwiches," enjoys a bite, 1955.
Centre: 1947/48 Rotary Club roster book sports an ad highlighting weekly Rotary luncheons at White Spot.
Bottom: Nat was known as a great supporter of both big and little leaguers.

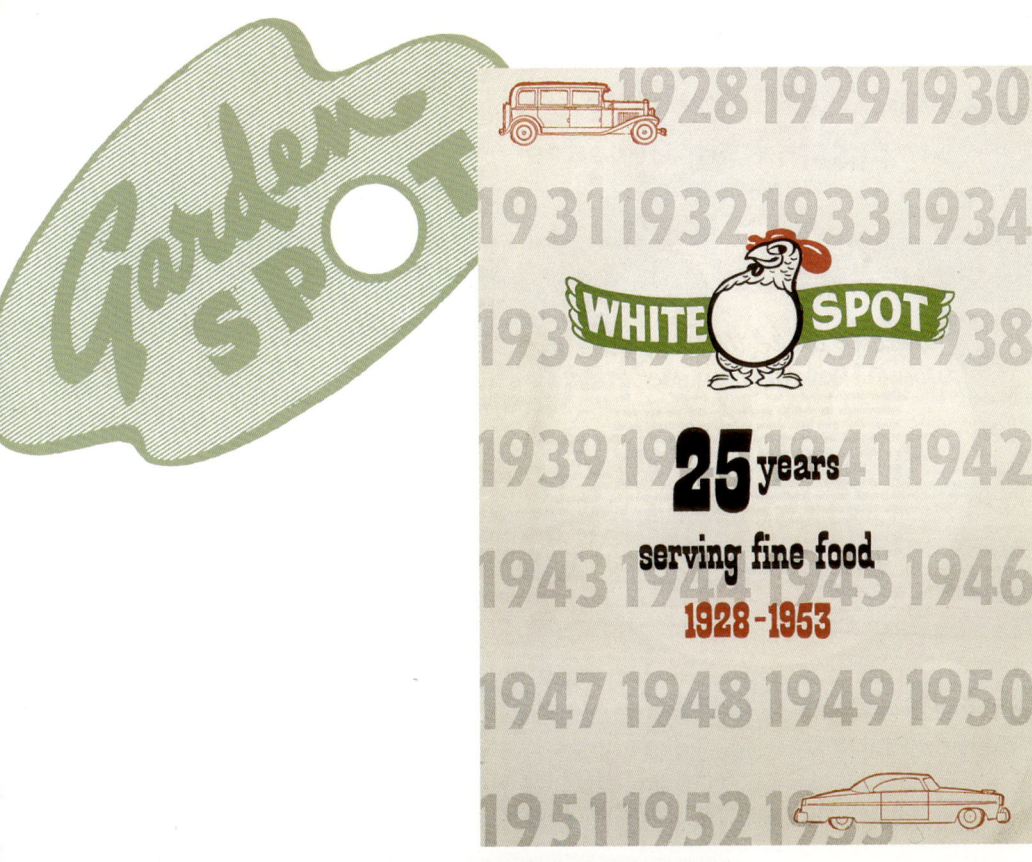

• White Spot's 25th anniversary booklet included a personal message of thanks and commitment from Eva and Nat to their guests.

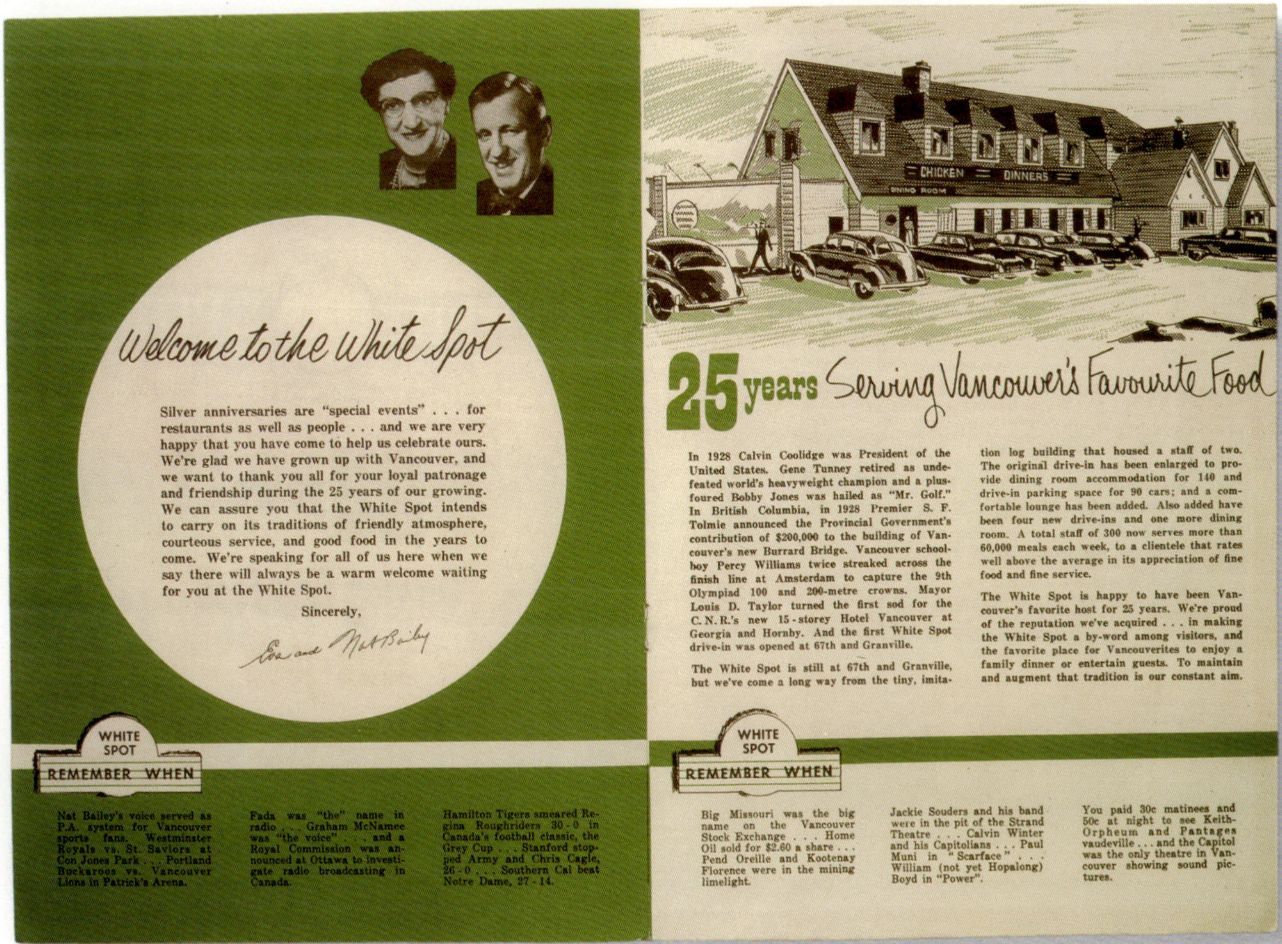

Welcome to the White Spot

Silver anniversaries are "special events" . . . for restaurants as well as people . . . and we are very happy that you have come to help us celebrate ours. We're glad we have grown up with Vancouver, and we want to thank you all for your loyal patronage and friendship during the 25 years of our growing. We can assure you that the White Spot intends to carry on its traditions of friendly atmosphere, courteous service, and good food in the years to come. We're speaking for all of us here when we say there will always be a warm welcome waiting for you at the White Spot.

Sincerely,

Eva and Nat Bailey

WHITE SPOT REMEMBER WHEN

Nat Bailey's voice served as P.A. system for Vancouver sports fans. Westminster Royals vs. St. Saviors at Con Jones Park . . . Portland Buckaroos vs. Vancouver Lions in Patrick's Arena.

Fada was "the" name in radio . . . Graham McNamee was "the voice" . . . and a Royal Commission was announced at Ottawa to investigate radio broadcasting in Canada.

Hamilton Tigers smeared Regina Roughriders 30-0 in Canada's football classic, the Grey Cup . . . Stanford stopped Army and Chris Cagle, 26-0 . . . Southern Cal beat Notre Dame, 27-14.

CHICKEN DINNERS

DINING ROOM

25 years Serving Vancouver's Favourite Food

In 1928 Calvin Coolidge was President of the United States. Gene Tunney retired as undefeated world's heavyweight champion and a plus-foured Bobby Jones was hailed as "Mr. Golf." In British Columbia, in 1928 Premier S. F. Tolmie announced the Provincial Government's contribution of $200,000 to the building of Vancouver's new Burrard Bridge. Vancouver schoolboy Percy Williams twice streaked across the finish line at Amsterdam to capture the 9th Olympiad 100 and 200-metre crowns. Mayor Louis D. Taylor turned the first sod for the C.N.R.'s new 15-storey Hotel Vancouver at Georgia and Hornby. And the first White Spot drive-in was opened at 67th and Granville.

The White Spot is still at 67th and Granville, but we've come a long way from the tiny, imitation log building that housed a staff of two. The original drive-in has been enlarged to provide dining room accommodation for 140 and drive-in parking space for 90 cars; and a comfortable lounge has been added. Also added have been four new drive-ins and one more dining room. A total staff of 300 now serves more than 60,000 meals each week, to a clientele that rates well above the average in its appreciation of fine food and fine service.

The White Spot is happy to have been Vancouver's favorite host for 25 years. We're proud of the reputation we've acquired . . . in making the White Spot a by-word among visitors, and the favorite place for Vancouverites to enjoy a family dinner or entertain guests. To maintain and augment that tradition is our constant aim.

WHITE SPOT REMEMBER WHEN

Big Missouri was the big name on the Vancouver Stock Exchange . . . Home Oil sold for $2.60 a share . . . Pend Oreille and Kootenay Florence were in the mining limelight.

Jackie Souders and his band were in the pit of the Strand Theatre . . . Calvin Winter and his Capitolians . . . Paul Muni in "Scarface" . . . William (not yet Hopalong) Boyd in "Power".

You paid 30c matinees and 50c at night to see Keith-Orpheum and Pantages vaudeville . . . and the Capitol was the only theatre in Vancouver showing sound pictures.

COURTESY OF WHITE SPOT

Six Fascinating Decades

If anyone knows the complete story of White Spot, it's Robert J. Stout. In 1934, a 17-year-old Bob and his brother Irwin joined the White Spot family. Six decades and three sets of ownership later, Bob retired. Today he remains White Spot's unofficial historian.

"My first job was selling peanuts and soft drinks at the Christmas Day hockey game at Denman Arena. We made more money, had more fun and saw more sports than we ever did delivering the morning papers."

Bob's first drive-in assignment came on a Saturday night in 1936. "White duck pants were the order of the day.... I was instructed to direct the drivers to park their cars close together and maximize the available space. I did a good job, as was attested by Tim O'Flaherty, another carhop, when he asked Nat for a clean uniform for Sunday. 'Why?' asked Nat. 'Because the new kid has packed the cars so closely that we cleaned them as we served them,' came the reply."

As the years passed, Bob became one of White Spot's five co-owners. He managed the opening of the company's $1.5-million commissary in 1958 and was instrumental in developing the unique White Spot trays. A born marketer, he came up with many inventive sales ideas, such as illuminated Read-o-graph signs, and scenic placemats of British Columbia beauty spots. As soon as they appeared, customers began collecting them: one per season for a set of four.

This spry ex-carhop remained with the company through the General Foods era (1968 - 1982) as vice-president of Corporate Affairs, and then part-time for several years under current owner Peter Toigo. "Working with White Spot was a very satisfactory part of my life. The company recognizes the importance of its employees. That's why so many of us stay for so long," Bob said.

• *Left:* Bob Stout, in 1937, when he was a carhop, cook and acting manager. *Right:* Partners Cecil Eustace, Nat, Bob Stout, Ernie Creamer, Art Jones and Roy Parkinson.

• In the 1950s Eva and Nat enjoyed occasional holiday breaks from business. Here they pose with the catch of the day.

• Pleasure was often combined with business. *Above:* Boating in the south. *Below:* Attending a restaurateurs' conference.

• In the 1960s, the Granville Dining Room drew an appreciative crowd. On this occasion, Nat, Eva and Bob Stout are among the diners.

"Slip in as You Slide By"

In the 1950s, White Spot's advertising agency, Goodwin Ellis, developed exterior signs, dubbed Read-o-graphs, as a simple but effective advertising device. The illuminated messages, outside each location except White Spot #1, were changed twice a week. Corny but catchy, they were written by Bob Stout with suggestions from customers and staff and often related to local news, sports or weather:

SLIP IN AS YOU SLIDE BY – January 18, 1954

FOR A LABOURLESS DAY DINE WITH US – August 30, 1954

SEVEN DAYS WITHOUT OUR HAMBURGER MAKES ONE WEAK – March 24, 1955

FIRST GREY CUP FOOTBALL GAME AT EMPIRE STADIUM – Nov. 21, 1955

BUY A SHARE IN YOUR TEAM DURING BASEBALL WEEK – January 4, 1957

AFTER THE SPORTSMAN'S SHOW FEED YOUR DEAR HERE – May 2, 1960

• *Above:* White Spot, New Westminster, 1960.
Below: White Spot, Burrard and Georgia, 1951.

Picture-Postcard Perfect

When artist David Tait painted a White Spot mural, people would drive over at lunch to eat and watch the show. Climbing atop a high stepladder, he created rugged mountains or pastoral countrysides with quick, clean brushstrokes. The giant images – each on a billboard up to eight feet high by 30 feet long – were pure British Columbia, from coastal scenes to Rocky Mountains, as famous with locals as the Sun Tower and the Lion's Gate Bridge. "Instead of having a plain fence, they gave the customers something colourful to look at," recalled David. "They were a real drawing card, the talk of the town."

The murals first appeared in the 1930s, the creations of local artists Jim Osborne and Pete Hopkinson. The most impressive display was at the Granville and 67th location where eight billboards lined the back of the Drive-in. Other White Spot drive-ins boasted from four to six panels. The murals were moved twice a year between locations, with new ones added on a regular basis.

Examples of these bygone days can still be seen at the White Spot at Georgia and Cardero streets and in New Westminster. Those with a taste for nostalgia and Triple-O are often found sitting in their cars in front of these giant postcards.

• White Spot's giant postcard murals were instantly renowned. *Top:* Artist Jim Osborne's son in front of the Rocky Mountain range. *Bottom:* Jim Osborne and one of his masterpieces.

the key to continued success. And in the spirit of this fast pace, White Spot opened the largest commissary in western Canada to prepare its food, expanded the Granville Street Dining Room, opened new locations in New Westminster and on SE Marine Dr. and brought ICL Services into the White Spot fold.

But the biggest news of all was the opening of the Oakridge Dining Room.

The Canadian Pacific Railway's Oakridge subdivision, 276 acres in all, was built in the mid-1950s. It included the $10-million Oakridge Shopping Centre and once again, White Spot was on the scene. Nat was on a roll, oblivious to the fact that this would prove to be one of his more challenging financial gambles. Ernie Creamer, Nat's right-hand man on the project, remembered, "The boss immediately said yes to a dining room, but even before it opened, Oakridge started getting out of control costwise."

At first, the sky was the limit. The new dining room was designed by Raymond, Inc. of Seattle, and boasted carpets specially woven in England, handcrafted chandeliers and table pedestals and a state-of-the-art all-stainless steel kitchen that was a chef's paradise. But building heaven on earth is expensive and in this case the bills added up to a staggering $250,000. Nat had high ambitions for the room; he wanted it to be more popular than the original White Spot Dining Room. "All restaurant guys who make it big have to build a monument to themselves, and Oakridge was Nat's," said Ernie. "It never made any money: it was just too costly."

Perhaps dreams are priceless, though, for the press enthused about "the fabulous Oakridge Room." Shortly before the May 6, 1959 opening, the *Vancouver Sun* gave its support to the venture: "The best peanut-pitching arm in Minor League baseball will throw open the doors to the finest restaurant on the Pacific Coast." The high praise was appreciated, but the Oakridge Room didn't quite fulfil Nat's dream. Yet today, in the renovated Oakridge

One of a Kind

Like many of White Spot's innovations, the Commissary, the company's food preparation centre, started small and grew and grew. Originally located in buildings behind the billboards at White Spot #1, the Commissary became a 4,000-square-foot giant by 1948. Cooks, bakers, butchers, delivery truck drivers, food preparers and supervisors collaborated in a daily challenge to provide fresh food to all White Spot kitchens.

The pie pantry was the star of the Commissary. By 1939, Nat had established the staple flavours: boysenberry, blueberry, apple, raspberry, and for special holidays, pumpkin and hot mincemeat. But pies were just one of a constellation of foods prepared daily. To ensure consistency, cooks in each location consulted colourful books illustrating the presentation of each dish.

In 1958, White Spot opened a new 27,000-square-foot commissary on SE Marine Dr., including offices and a restaurant. The Commissary doubled in size in 1968, was expanded again in 1990 and renamed Granville House in honour of the original White Spot #1.

From day one, the Commissary promised the finest of fresh foods and defied the industry trend toward processed products. White Spot still makes food today the way Nat and Eva originally intended: fresh, unique-tasting and of premium quality.

• **Quality control tour of the Commissary, 1974.**

A True Sportsman

Capilano Stadium, one of the finest ball diamonds in North American baseball in the 1950s, cried out for a resident club. In 1956, Nat and a group of local businessmen bought the Oakland Oaks, moved them north and renamed them the Vancouver Mounties, one of eight triple-A teams in the Pacific Coast League.

Local business and civic leaders were behind the purchase, encouraging fans to buy $25 shares in the team; even Premier W.A.C. Bennett bought a share.

Although the public dug deeply for its pennies, it was Nat who kept the team afloat. He stuck by the financially troubled club as president until 1960, and as honorary president in 1961. His contributions continued until the team shut down for good in 1969.

As writer Jim Kearney recalled in 1985, "Nat Bailey was not an athlete, but he was one of the best friends Vancouver sport has ever had. Just what the game of baseball in Vancouver owes him nobody will ever really know, for he made a point of never broadcasting the number of times he went into his own pocket."

Triple-A ball would return in 1978 in the form of the Vancouver Canadians. That same year, "Mr. B's" contribution to baseball was honoured when the Capilano Brewing Company renamed their park the Nat Bailey Stadium.

• The 1959 Vancouver Mounties pose for their team photo. *Inset:* Nat, president, and Cedric Tallis, general manager.

• Nat was essential to triple-A baseball in Vancouver and in the 1950s was part owner of the Mounties. Their official score books reside in tthe B.C. Hall of Fame.

Under the Famous Peaked Cap

What most people remember about White Spot uniforms is the celebrated peaked cap once worn by every carhop. Adorned with the server's nametag, it had a tendency to fall off or sit crooked on the head but nonetheless it was the emblem of the honourable car server – and sometimes the object of teenage pranksters who would drive in, pluck one from a startled carhop, and speed off into the night.

The uniforms have changed over the years. During the war, "girl hops" wore the same white pants and shirts of their male predecessors, complete with the signature peaked caps. After the war, White Spot moved to the more modern green and white uniforms – the company colours of the time. The outer uniforms came in summer and winter fabrics which were always worn with white shirts of high quality cotton.

Today's uniform sports a pastel-striped shirt with a teal skirt for women while the men wear a classic combination of black pants and white shirt. The uniforms have changed, but the playful spirit and assurance of quality once represented by that famous peaked cap are still alive today in the men and women who serve the guests of the White Spot family.

- *Above:* The famous peaked cap, worn by White Spot carhops in the 1950s. *Below:* After the war, male carhops reappeared. This 1949 photo includes Bob Stout (fourth from left) and Cecil Eustace (second from right).

Shopping Mall, an elegant, affordable White Spot family restaurant now thrives, with rarely an empty table in sight.

In spite of change, in spite of increasing financial gambles, White Spot still paid attention to the little touches that made the restaurants memorable for their guests. In the summer of 1959, SMILE bumper stickers and pocket-sized calendars were introduced, distributed by the thousands to White Spot customers. These ingenious items, in retrospect, echoed a simpler time when an open personality, eager perseverance and personal contacts were the essence of an entrepreneur. For Nat, the old days of business in Vancouver – when deals were sealed with a handshake and a promise – were drawing to a close. As the 1960s approached, new styles were emerging. The next decade would herald the sunset years for the amiable paper boy from Minnesota and the start of a significantly new era for White Spot. •

• **Top:** In 1959, White Spot's PNE float conveyed both Nat's belief in growing with the times and his love of baseball.
Bottom: Smiling from the '50s through the '70s. From top to bottom: a hockey schedule, bumper sticker, wallet card and button.

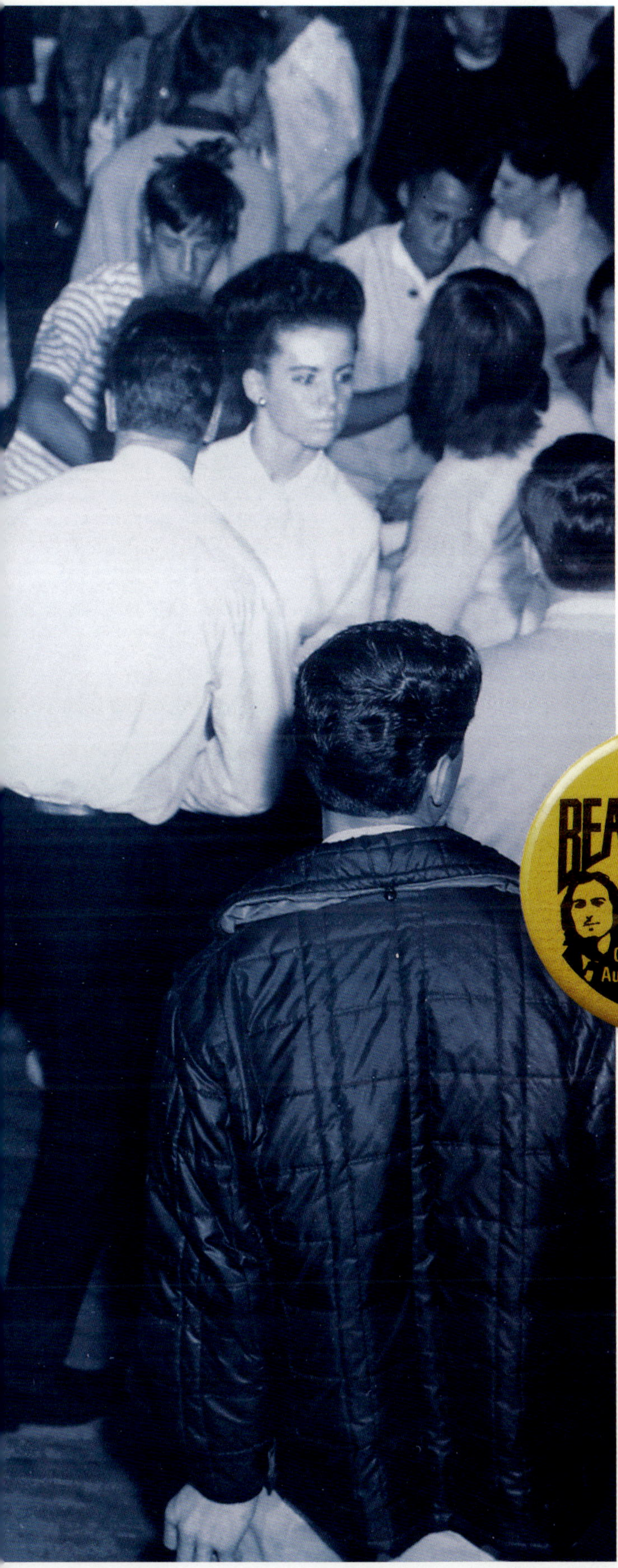

1960-1982 The Transition Years

In the 1960s, the decade of youth, the Triple-O burger was as popular as the Beatles with British Columbia teenagers.

A White Spot drive-in was the "in" place to congregate: kids crammed into their parents' cars for an evening cruise and topped it off at White Spot. Yet Mother's Day was the most popular day of the year, with cars lined up around the block, their passengers patiently waiting for a parking spot. The White Spot family, now comprised of 10 locations, embraced the new decade with confidence and enthusiasm.

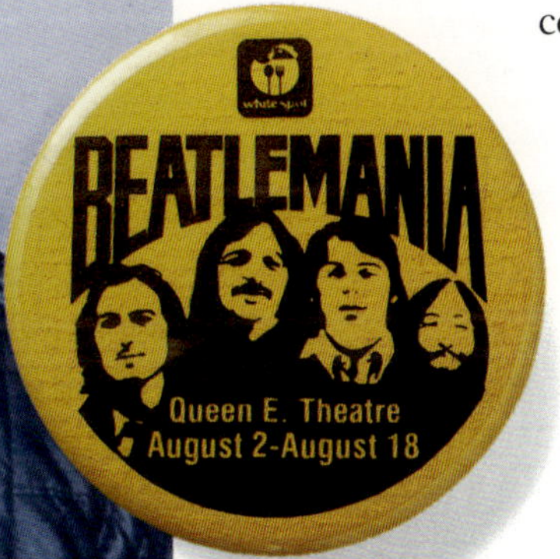

The company was nearing its 40th anniversary, and there was no slowing down. In 1960, at a Canadian Restaurant Association convention in Toronto, Nat Bailey's five associate partners were sold on the merits of Kentucky Fried Chicken (KFC) and encouraged White Spot to buy KFC franchise rights for British Columbia. Nat had met Colonel Sanders, the creator of KFC, many times at earlier conventions and respected the Colonel's product and his consummate sales abilities. Still, Nat was skeptical at first. "If you want to promote chicken, promote our own product, Chicken in the Straw."

Within a year, however, Nat agreed that Kentucky Fried Chicken was a unique product with an exciting sales potential. He agreed to let his partners create a separate company, Ernie's Fine Foods, to take on the KFC franchise. With Colonel Sanders in attendance, the first three KFC stores opened in the Lower

• *Facing page:* New dances for a new decade: B.C. teens at the PNE, 1963. *Above:* White Spot meets Beatlemania.

Triple-O Love

Since the very beginning, White Spot has inspired romance. Starting with Nat and Eva Bailey, dozens of couples met and married while working for the company. Three of Nat's five partners, including dedicated bachelor Cecil Eustace, met their mates this way. And it wasn't only employees who were smitten. The drive-in was perfect for courting. "In the 1930s and 1940s, we'd drive slowly up there, have a meal and drive slowly back," recalled longtime customer Mildred Wylie. "It was a precious chance to be alone."

By the 1960s, love and White Spot were almost synonymous, particularly for teenagers like Phil Bayley. The 16-year-old started as a carhop at the Gilmore White Spot in 1962, and for the next five years, Phil combined school with evening and weekend shifts at the drive-in.

However, Phil's first attempt at impressing a girl, a White Spot customer, proved calamitous. "It was comical in a way," remembered Phil, today a sales representative for Broadway Printers. "She arrived with her family, six people in the car, and they ordered a huge meal. I came out carrying two extremely heavy trays, one up over my head and the other by my side. While I was passing between two cars, one tray clipped the antenna of the car beside theirs. I lost everything off both trays."

A better impression was made when the daughter of co-worker Mary Cosman started at "The Spot" as a waitress. "Her mother had told me Bette was too old for me. But as it turned out, she was only a year older." Phil and Bette went out together for three years, were engaged and later happily married — a true Triple-O romance that carries on today.

Mainland in 1961. The Colonel's celebrity status, combined with low-priced introductory offers, sparked two days of extraordinary line-ups at the new KFC outlets. By 1993, when KFC was sold to Pepsico to allow White Spot Limited to focus on its restaurant division, the franchise was so popular it had grown to 67 locations in B.C.

The establishment of Ernie's Fine Foods was only one of several expansion moves. The White Spot at Lougheed Hwy. and Gilmore Ave. opened in 1961, destined to become one of the company's most popular drive-ins. "Teenagers used to live at the drive-in," recalled Frank Krische, a 43-year White Spot employee. Carloads of young people dropped by for burgers en route to the Pacific National Exhibition, football and hockey games or on the way home from the movies. "It was definitely the place to hang out," said Frank, who was the senior assistant at Lougheed and Gilmore in the mid-1960s and later a general manager there for ten years.

Several months after that location was launched, the first "overseas" White Spot opened at the Victoria Town and Country Shopping Centre. At first, Victoria's residents eyed the city's first drive-in with some suspicion. However, as with all the White Spots

• In 1965 the SMILE! campaign included the Nat Bailey Villa Hotel.

• A beaming Colonel Sanders arrives in Campbell River in 1973 to open the KFC location there, accompanied by (left to right): pilot, Ernie Creamer, Peter Main, Al Jeske and Vince Simpson.

"Overseas" with White Spot

White Spot's big news of 1961 was the opening of its restaurant at the Victoria Town and Country Shopping Centre in Saanich, a short drive from downtown Victoria. Knowing that the "overseas" White Spot, as it was nicknamed, would be the first of many locations outside the Lower Mainland, White Spot sent key staff members to open the new restaurant, including partner Roy Parkinson as manager.

Since then, the number of White Spots outside the Lower Mainland has grown to nine. In many ways, Karen Grey, general manager of the Nanaimo White Spot, is typical of the loyal employees outside the Lower Mainland. After graduating from British Columbia Institute of Technology's Hospitality Program, she joined the company in 1988. Starting as a server, she was promoted to manager and then general manager within five years. Today, the 150-seat White Spot she manages serves about 6,400 customers a week, many of whom are visitors to the city.

Students from nearby Malaspina College and other schools make up a significant part of Karen's staff of 65 full- and part-time employees. The staff work hard, know how to have fun and contribute happily to their community. During Nanaimo's annual Marine Festival, they go all-out, wearing Bathtub Race t-shirts, giving out gift certificates and sponsoring Silly Boat and Wader races. Supporting the community is as much a part of White Spot as is its celebrated cheesecake, and Karen is proud of the efforts of her newer employees as well as her long-time staff members (many have worked with the company for over 10 years) — all serve White Spot's famous food with a warm smile and a hot tip about the excellent fishing just up the coast.

• *Left:* The modern interior of the Victoria White Spot. *Above:* The first White Spot restaurant outside the Lower Mainland.

The Story of Pirate Pak

• **Treasure-laden Pirate Paks continue to lure hungry young brigands.**

In the 1960s, family restaurants were increasingly popular and competition among them was fierce. Fortunately, White Spot was high up on the list of family favourites. It seemed that almost every car coming into a White Spot drive-in needed two trays, one in the front for mom and dad and one in the back for the kids. Customers wanted a reasonably priced family meal and menu items that appealed to children — and they got both at White Spot.

On Saturday, July 23, 1968, carhops dressed as pirates appeared at every White Spot to promote the launch of the Pirate Pak to a receptive audience. A child's full meal, complete with a chocolate doubloon, was served in a colourful cardboard pirate ship.

As with today's menu, children could choose from a smaller version of the Legendary Hamburger, hot dog, macaroni and cheese, grilled cheese sandwich, fish 'n' chips or chicken, served with a beverage and soft ice cream.

The Pirate Pak was an immediate hit with kids, and its galleon design became so recognizable that the company commissioned a replica for a float which appeared in the PNE parade and other community parades throughout British Columbia. Such popularity could scarcely be improved upon, so changes have been minor, White Spot now offering options such as vegetables instead of french fries. Nonetheless, the success of the original is undiminished: 425,000 young pirates a year swing by for a Pak.

Goodbye, Mr. Baseball

to local sports lovers he was "Mr. Baseball." Within the business community, he was known as a regular guy who actively supported local groups like the Marpole Rotary, the Shriners, the Masons and the Chamber of Commerce. To the people who worked for him, he was known as Mr. B, The Old Man, Dad, or Mr. Bailey, never "Nat" which was the privilege of his few close friends.

It was said he loved the colour green because it was the colour of money. But rather than hoard his hard-won earnings, he was generous to a fault. He dug into his pocket countless times and gave without stinting to his beloved baseball, from professional to little leagues. His office door was always open and he helped dozens of people get into business. When, with a little of his financial help, they did succeed, he would smile his engaging smile and remain silent about his role in their success. Essentially a quiet man, Nat kept his feelings to himself.

After leaving White Spot Limited in 1968, Nat found he couldn't retire to the "quiet life" — it wasn't his style to die of boredom. Instead, he started a second career investing in hotels and condominiums. Right to the end he never slowed down.

On March 27, 1978, "Mr. B" passed away in Vancouver General Hospital at the age of 76. Nat Bailey may have too often been described as a self-made man. He became what he was, in part because of a fan's fascination with baseball, and due to relentless hard work. But his main motivation was love — for the people who made up his ever-increasing White Spot family. And the hundreds who thronged his memorial service to honour him at Kerrisdale Presbyterian Church were evidence of that fact.

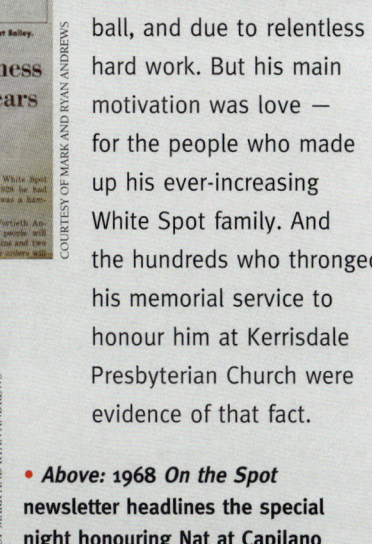

• *Above:* 1968 *On the Spot* newsletter headlines the special night honouring Nat at Capilano Stadium. *Left:* "Mr. Baseball" in 1961.

Pipe Up the Band

It was 1963, and seven years after forming the Optimist Junior Pipe Band, Don Bellamy found himself contemplating the demise of his group. Although the young pipers were enthusiastic, money was scarce and the Optimists could no longer support a travelling band that was by now in demand across B.C. and as far afield as Hawaii. In December, at a Christmas party, Don mentioned to White Spot partner Bob Stout that the future of the pipe band was in danger.

Together, the two men approached Nat Bailey to ask him to sponsor the band and allow it to use the White Spot name. At first, he was reluctant: "He liked to help without fanfare," recalled Don. Finally Nat, who was a fan of the band, relented and the group became the White Spot Pipe Band and Highland Dancers.

The 50-member band, made up of male and female pipers aged 10 to 15, has won first prizes in most major parades including the Pacific National Exhibition, Seattle Seafair and Honolulu Fair. It was one of the first pipe bands to tour Central Mexico, and "most certainly one of the first pipe bands to play in the Torch Light Parade at the Quebec City Winter Carnival with temperatures below minus 40," said Don.

In 1992, Don, the executive director of the Restaurant & Foodservices Association of B.C. and a Vancouver alderman, appointed Kim Chisholm as his Bandmaster but continues to act as the band's manager on White Spot's behalf. The White Spot Pipe Band and Highland Dancers keeps marching on, and along with its patron, continues to collect accolades and awards.

• **The White Spot Junior Pipe Band poses in front of Vancouver's renowned Marine Building.**

• White Spot annually acknowledges its most proficient outlets. *Above:* An award plaque bestowed on one of its coffee shops in 1969.

opened in the 1960s, it didn't take long for guests to come around. In June 1964, the company made another significant move, purchasing the bankrupt Villa Motor Hotel in Burnaby for $1,155,000 in cash and changing its name to the Nat Bailey Villa Hotel.

Behind the scenes, the partners were consolidating their assets. In April of 1967, White Spot's two company groups — one owned by Nat, the other by his five partners, with Nat as president of both — were merged, leaving Nat holding more than 50 percent of the shares. Then, in a surprise move after many years of refusing to consider outside offers of purchase, Nat suddenly announced that he had sold White Spot Limited to a major Eastern conglomerate. On April 1, 1968, Nat completed the sale of his 40-year-old company to General Foods, Limited for $6.5 million.

Perhaps it was the significant milestone of White Spot's 40th anniversary, Nat's age of 66 at the time, or the illness of his wife Eva that encouraged the sale. The company's public statement was that White Spot was sold to alleviate succession duty taxes. "My partners and I want to realize cash to set up our estates," he told the press. But whatever his reason for selling, the founder of White Spot wasn't about to retire. He continued going to the office every day in his new combined roles as president of the White Spot group and a vice-president of General Foods. He also continued to manage the Nat Bailey Villa Hotel, the one property he hadn't sold to the new owners.

White Spot's entry into the General Foods years, from 1968 to 1982, could be compared to a space ship launch. The message from the new owners was loud and clear: "Ladies and gentlemen, we're going into orbit. Hang onto your seats," announced a General Foods' vice-president. New construction, new systems, new packaging: these things would be done differently as General Foods brought White Spot into the modern era. "We can't stop change, any more than we can push toothpaste back into a tube," advised the vice-president.

The purchase of White Spot gave the Toronto-based company a solid-gold restaurant chain in Western Canada to complement its Canterbury Foods operation in Ontario. Included in the sale were 11 White Spot drive-ins, two dining rooms, six Ernie's Fine Foods outlets, contracts held by ICL Services, and Newton Farms, the largest private chicken farm in the province.

One of the top eight food purveyors in North America, General Foods accelerated White Spot's growth and modernization. Within a year of the purchase, the new owners announced a major

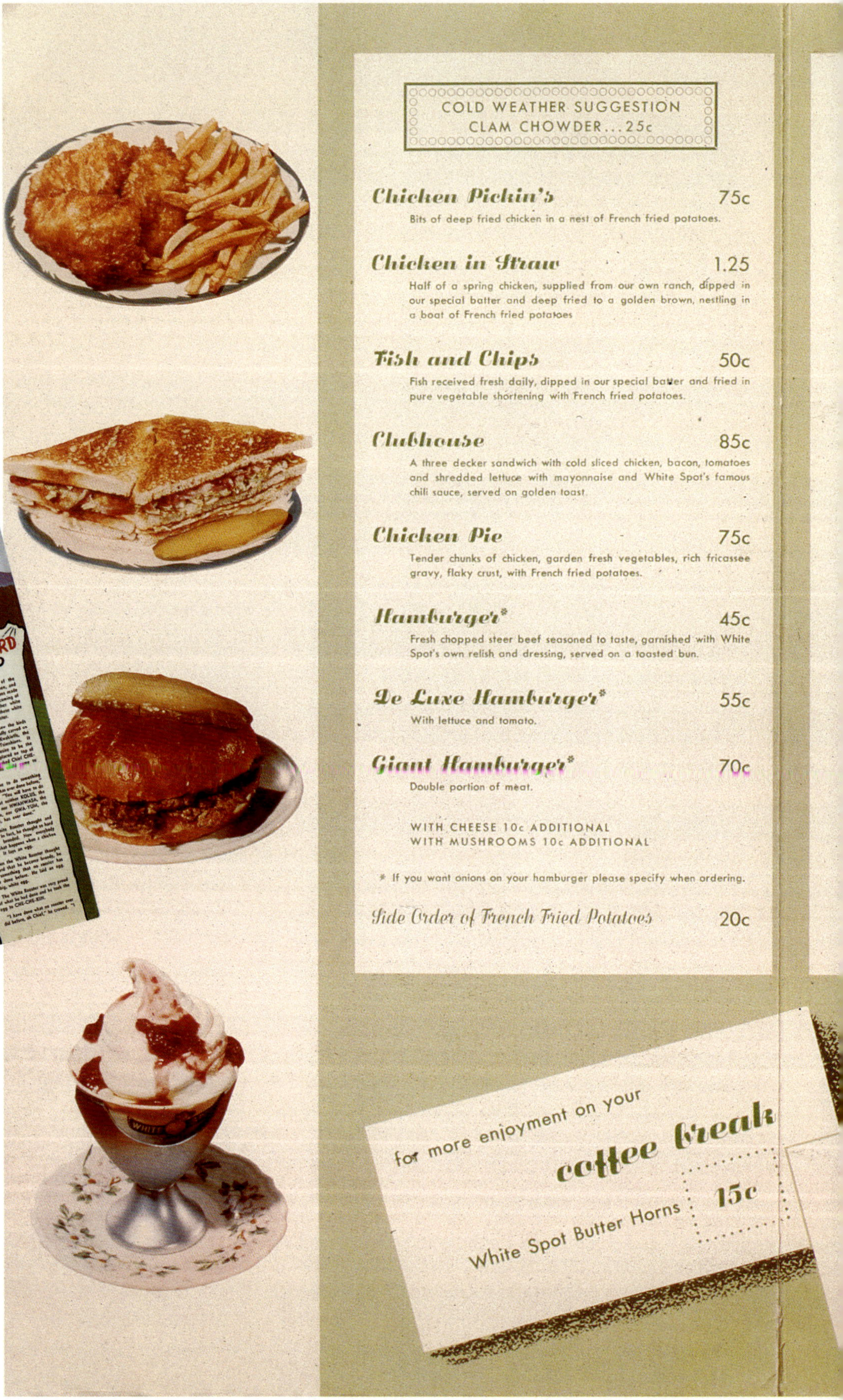

COLD WEATHER SUGGESTION
CLAM CHOWDER...25c

Chicken Pickin's 75c
Bits of deep fried chicken in a nest of French fried potatoes.

Chicken in Straw 1.25
Half of a spring chicken, supplied from our own ranch, dipped in our special batter and deep fried to a golden brown, nestling in a boat of French fried potatoes

Fish and Chips 50c
Fish received fresh daily, dipped in our special batter and fried in pure vegetable shortening with French fried potatoes.

Clubhouse 85c
A three decker sandwich with cold sliced chicken, bacon, tomatoes and shredded lettuce with mayonnaise and White Spot's famous chili sauce, served on golden toast.

Chicken Pie 75c
Tender chunks of chicken, garden fresh vegetables, rich fricassee gravy, flaky crust, with French fried potatoes.

Hamburger* 45c
Fresh chopped steer beef seasoned to taste, garnished with White Spot's own relish and dressing, served on a toasted bun.

De Luxe Hamburger* 55c
With lettuce and tomato.

Giant Hamburger* 70c
Double portion of meat.

WITH CHEESE 10c ADDITIONAL
WITH MUSHROOMS 10c ADDITIONAL

* If you want onions on your hamburger please specify when ordering.

Side Order of French Fried Potatoes 20c

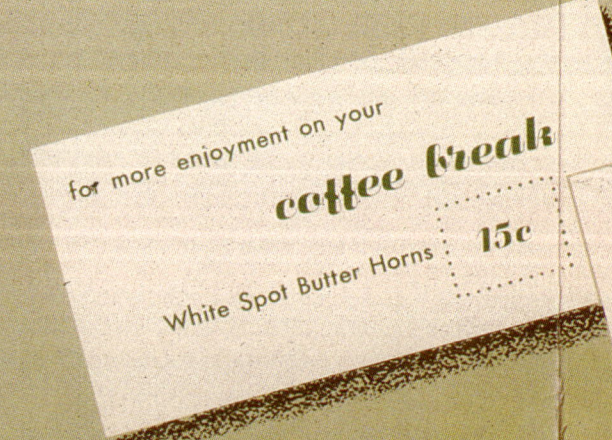

for more enjoyment on your
coffee break
White Spot Butter Horns 15c

COURTESY OF PHIL BAYLEY

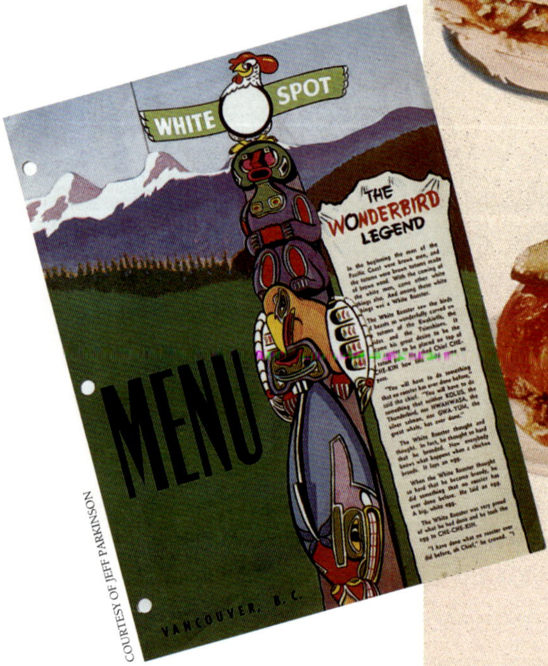

COURTESY OF JEFF PARKINSON

• ***Full page:*** **A 1955 menu includes numerous culinary delights, a catering service and Nat's Hall of Fame award by *American Restaurant* magazine. *Inset:* The fanciful story of *The Wonderbird Legend* is featured on a menu from the same era.**

COLD SANDWICHES

ken Sandwich	50c	Ham Sandwich	35c
Sandwich	45c	Cheese Sandwich	30c
	Lettuce and Tomato Sandwich	25c	

HOT SANDWICHES

ecued Chicken on Toasted Bun	50c	Bacon and Egg Sandwich	50c
ecued Beef on Toasted Bun	45c	Bacon Sandwich	40c
ed Ham and Cheese Sandwich	50c	Bacon and Mushroom Sandwich	50c
ed Ham Sandwich (A ham sandwich d in butter to a golden brown)	35c	Bacon and Tomato Sandwich	45c
		Side Order French Fried Potatoes	20c
ed Cheese Sandwich (A cheese wich grilled in butter to a golden brown)	30c	Cinnamon Toast	15c
d Egg Sandwich	30c	Brown or White Toast with Jam	15c

DESSERTS

from our own ovens, per cut	20c
with Soft Ice Cream	30c
Ice Cream	15c
colate Sundaes	25c
Frozen Strawberry Sundae	25c
AWBERRY SHORTCAKE WITH T ICE CREAM	30c
ESE CAKE	35c

HOT & COLD DRINKS

Milk Shakes, assorted flavors	25c
Milk Shakes with Malt	30c
Pot of Tea	10c
Coffee	10c
Hot Chocolate	15c
Milk	10c
Coca-Cola or Orange	10c
Tomato or Apple Juice	15c

"HALL OF FAME" PLAQUE
PRESENTED TO NAT BAILEY BY
THE AMERICAN RESTAURANT
MAGAZINE

TE DINING ROOMS
DATION FOR PARTIES OF 20-80
mbie at 25th Avenue
TRINITY 6-2545

Always a Friendly Smile

As White Spot expanded and introduced new restaurants, hostesses became an important part of business. In the early days, most were chosen by Eva Bailey, who had a particularly good instinct for choosing the right person for the role. First and foremost, she looked for someone who showed grace under pressure. Hosts and hostesses today follow in Eva's footsteps, personally welcoming guests and seating them when a table is available. If there is a rush or the restaurant is short-staffed, they help take orders and clean tables.

Geraldine "Gerry" Cooper started at the Kingsway and Gladstone White Spot in 1960. After 21 years working in the kitchen, she was asked to help out as a hostess at the W. Broadway and Larch St. White Spot. "The manager thought it would be a good idea to have an older influence around all the young girls on staff. I tried it and discovered I really enjoyed being a hostess," Gerry recalled. Today she works part-time. "I'm not ready to quit, not even after 12 years. I like people and I want to be among them. You really get to know everybody when you seat people."

And among those she seats are the occasionally difficult children, but it's a task Gerry accomplishes with aplomb. Recently she received a letter of commendation from the mother of rambunctious twin boys who was amazed that Gerry could calm them. "Mom," as she is known by customers and staff, keeps this letter in a scrapbook documenting life with her family — the White Spot family.

- Vancouver youth have always flocked to White Spot for the legendary satisfaction of good food, good times and good friends.

• Vancouver had many attractions in the 1970s, as it does today. *Top:* Kitsilano's Vanier Park. *Below:* Granville Street's Theatre Row.

development plan to enable its restaurants to keep pace with the expanding market in fast foods. In its prospectus were five new KFC locations and two new White Spot drive-ins plus the expansion of the existing White Spot at West Broadway and Larch St.

Nat had never been averse to growth, but his old-fashioned handshake style of management did not mesh with General Foods' modern approach. After several months he left to form a new hotel management company, Bailey Hotels Ltd., a role that would occupy him until his death in 1978.

After Nat's departure from White Spot Limited, the company continued with its expansion plans. To provide for its new acquisitions, it enlarged and updated the White Spot commissary, now called Quality Kitchens, until it was the most sophisticated food service operation in North America.

White Spot would also have a modern new look. Gone was the original green and red cockerel on White Spot's logo, replaced by an updated design of a chicken head. By 1977, hewn cedar signs, hanging flower baskets and indirect lighting appeared in nine new locations and five renovations of existing restaurants.

With White Spot as its base, General Foods was

• To promote the 1979 grand opening of the Guildford White Spot, Bob Stout chauffeurs a 1934 Dodge Roadster, with young Christopher Lane, restaurant manager Sal de Blasio (rear left) and serving then-president David Lane (rear right) is carhop David Dawe.

• **Above:** This group of happy kiddieland patrons, both young and old, testifies to the fact that Vancouver *is* family fun.

all set to build a national food system across Canada. With these ambitious goals, however, came a new set of tensions. From 1975 to 1978, the company faced a series of walk outs and strikes by White Spot employees, but harmony was finally returned when new contracts were approved.

As the 1970s neared an end, competition in the fast food and family restaurant markets was increasingly cutthroat. In the fall of 1979, General Foods established three task forces to analyse its future needs. One of these was a long-range strategy and organization study on new directions and new areas of business activity for the 1980s. As a result, White Spot Limited began shedding its fast-food image for a more formal one. Licensed restaurants began replacing coffee shops and by April 1982, White Spot Limited operated 28 White Spot restaurants as well as two top-of-the-line dinner houses, Granville House and the Oakridge Dining Room, 44 KFC outlets and 35 ICL Services contracts. More than 2,800 people were on its payroll, with approximately 1,500 working at White Spot restaurants.

General Foods pursued expansion and excellence, introducing up-to-the-minute management and accounting systems from their eastern base in Ontario while learning how B.C. did business. A succession of four White Spot presidents carried out the General Foods' expansion: Brian Laragh, Peter T. Main, David C. Lane and Ron Tomlinson. The B.C. operations were profitable, with combined sales of about $100 million in 1981 — but General Foods was not as lucky with its U.S. restaurant ventures, which were losing money. As a result of its weakened position, it decided to sell its restaurant divisions in both the U.S. and Canada, including its White Spot holdings.

At this crucial time in White Spot's history, Peter C. Toigo, then a little-known B.C. entrepreneur and land developer, began to seriously consider the possibility of buying White Spot. He had known and admired Nat Bailey, another self-made man, and had followed the company's progress under General Foods. "The truth is I always wanted to buy White Spot but I had no idea that it was even up for sale," said Peter. Prompted by the suggestion of a business associate, he decided to pick up the phone and inquire. His timely telephone call would soon result in White Spot's returning to British Columbian hands. •

• More promotional buttons from the White Spot collection.

Drive-in Memories

As a teenager, I didn't trust any restaurant that wouldn't bring food out to your car. In fact, I couldn't imagine anything more elegant than flashing your headlights at the White Spot drive-in. In those days, the carhops wore caps that made them look like policemen in aprons. They would slide the slots of an endless tray into the window ledge of my father's Oldsmobile until it was parallel to my Adam's apple. Even as I grew past the towering milkshakes, I thought carhopping seemed like one of the noblest professions in the city.

"If Vancouver were a girl, she'd be the one I caught a glimpse of at the White Spot somewhere in the heat of 1967. . . . She was about 16, which qualified her as a much older woman at the time. The kind of girl who wears the beach, and everything that surrounds it, the way other people slip into a tailored jacket. . . . But it's hard to recall all the details, probably because she was feeding a piece of strawberry pie to a raccoon who sat contentedly in the back window.

"I can remember the way she smiled at me to this day. And, for months, I had the fantasy of discovering her years later. I would be an older, much taller carhop assigned to deliver a piece of strawberry pie to a somewhat rusty Chevrolet. The window would descend slowly to reveal an arthritic raccoon and the woman of my dreams."

— **John Lekich,** first published in *Vancouver Magazine,* December 1992

1982-1993 Being the Best

In the fall of 1982, General Foods, Limited was looking for a buyer for the food services end of its business, which included all of its White Spot Limited holdings. Most, if not all, offers were expected to come from large companies. It was only with reluctance that Robert W. Hiller, controller of General Foods, Limited accepted a call late in the business day from an unknown British Columbia entrepreneur, Peter C. Toigo, who wanted to discuss White Spot and the possibility of purchasing it. Intrigued, Bob agreed to meet him after hours in General Foods' nearly empty Toronto executive offices. As luck would have it, after only a few minutes, the two men established a rapport. A few weeks later, a handshake deal was reached regarding the sale of the company, at a price of $38 million.

Securing the financing was a greater challenge. Peter Toigo readily admits that the sale came close to collapsing numerous times. More than once, Bob Hiller's colleagues and investment bankers recommended that he terminate the deal and find another buyer. It was only Bob's stubborn faith in Peter's ability to complete the financing that stopped him from acting on their advice.

In White Spot's first days, Nat Bailey had taken a chance and written a cheque for $11. Now the stakes had climbed into the multi-millions and the final closing of the sale had "one last cardiac-level hiccup," recalled Bob. While a roomful of lawyers waited, Peter called him out of the meeting, calmly telling the General Foods controller that he was still short a million dollars but he expected to have it within a few days. On Bob's advice, General Foods agreed to guarantee the missing million for the few days needed. The money did indeed arrive in good time, and by the end of December 1982, White Spot became part of Shato Holdings Limited, the company Peter had formed in 1969.

The sale of White Spot Limited included 24 White Spots, 54 KFC outlets, ICL Services catering contracts and Ontario-based Crock & Block restaurants. "I got property I never even knew was in the deal," Peter said later.

After 15 years, ownership of White Spot Limited was once again in the hands of a B.C. resident. Like Nat Bailey before him, Peter Toigo was an inventive and risk-taking entrepreneur who began making business deals as a pre-teen.

A committed family man, he believed in putting his wife and six children first and keeping a low public profile. Buying White Spot, a dream he pursued against the advice of his business advisors, would soon put him very much in the public eye.

Born in Powell River, B.C. in 1932, Peter Toigo's greatest influences were his family. Both his parents were immigrants from Northern Italy. His mother, Carmella, had arrived in Canada at age two and his father, Ernie, as a teenager. They lived across the street from Peter's grandparents. By the age of four, young

• **Peter Toigo embodies the values of a small community and a close-knit family.** *Left:* Peter and his dog Spotty at Kurple's Store in Powell River in the late 1930s. *Facing page:* Peter's first communion photograph.

Above: Peter with his parents, Carmella and Ernie.
Below right: Peter, age seven, in front of his grandfather's delivery truck.

Pete was already working, riding atop the horse his grandfather would hire out to plough the neighbours' fields. By the time he was seven, Peter was selling chickens and eggs door-to-door, driving around with his grandfather in a little Morris Minor truck to make deliveries.

It was in these early years that Peter learned the elements of success — hard work, courage, innovation and honesty, but above all, service to one's clients. Later, he would tell his children who followed him into business, "Make sure you look after your customers. Always do the best job you can, and never worry too much about the competition."

While still attending Powell River High School, Peter's positive approach to life made him the boy most likely to succeed. He already had several businesses on the go, from collecting empty beer bottles for the refunds to selling grapes to local winemakers. It was not unusual for a teacher to tell the young entrepreneur that there was a long-distance telephone call for him, usually from truckers having trouble at the Canada-U.S. border. He also made part-time money working shifts at a gas station and at the MacMillan Bloedel lumber mill.

In 1949, 17-year-old Peter and his parents combined their resources and bought the Wildwood Grocery Store in Wildwood, a suburb of Powell River. The following year was also a momentous one for the young man. Although only 18, he married his high school sweetheart — a marriage still going strong — and completed his first major land development transaction with the purchase of the Westview Dairy Company. "I went around to see the owner about buying a single lot from him," said Peter, "and discovered he was ill and could barely do his work. He needed help, so I stayed for the day. I ended up buying the whole dairy, herd, land and all, because the owner trusted me with only a small down payment." Even Peter's parents, by now well acquainted with their son's adventurous business spirit, wondered if he could pull off his plan of subdividing the land into lots, but he did and made a tidy profit.

For more than a decade, the Wildwood Grocery Store would be Peter's "office." While he worked there as a butcher, he had many enterprising sidelines on the go: he serviced vending machines, built houses on an Indian reserve, invested in grapes and even erected

• Young and well on his way: Peter and his first car, a Ford Model A, in front of his grandmother's house.

outhouses on Savary Island. He was also the first person to sell televisions and appliances in Powell River.

In 1960, the 28-year-old Peter took another major gamble with the purchase of downtown Powell River from the MacMillan Bloedel lumber company. "It was a simple formula, according to Peter," recalled Don Jones, whose company assisted in the financing of the sale. "MacMillan Bloedel wanted to sell its houses and commercial sites and Peter felt buying the company town would not be a problem for him. It was the first of a series of successful land deals we did together." As a joke, Peter always appeared on the financing company's applications as "occupation - meat cutter."

The following year, he built the Surfrider Apartments and the Plaza Shopping Centre, the first major shopping centre in the town. Although he continued to develop property in Powell River, building two more shopping centres, a hotel, motel and townhouses, Peter was already expanding his horizons. Three years later, he moved his growing family to Delta, B.C., a 40-minute drive from downtown Vancouver. By now he was buying and developing

• **Right: In 1988 White Spot and Science World brought *Dinosaurs!* to the people of Vancouver.**

A Fan for Life

Jim Pattison — chairman and president of the Expo 86 Corporation during the exciting six months of Vancouver's world's fair — is a longtime White Spot customer. "The White Spot Dining Room on Granville St. was the best place to eat in town. During the 1940s, I went there every Sunday after church with my parents. All the church crowd would be there dressed to the teeth. Then when I got married, my wife and I did the same thing with our children. I went to that White Spot for at least 20 years.

"When I first started doing business at my car dealership on Cambie St., I ate at the White Spot at Cambie and 25th every day of my life except Sundays. I always had the same thing — Legendary Platter and a chocolate milkshake — and I never got tired of it.

"Some time later, if I was on the way to the airport for a night flight east on business, I would always stop at White Spot and have a good steak, with mashed potatoes and ketchup, baking powder biscuits and greengage jam. These days, I still go there a couple of times a week.

"White Spot really is part of our history; it's a tradition. Other restaurants have appeared but they can't knock it out. Instead, White Spot just gets stronger. And the food is as good as ever."

Making a Difference

White Spot has always fused Nat Bailey's love of sports with his sense of community spirit. Prince George offers a prime example. There, White Spot sponsors a three-day triple-A bantam hockey tournament, a minor girls' "Mites" softball team and acts as the booster club for the Prince George Spruce Kings Junior A hockey club. Further south in Surrey, White Spot supports the annual Pacific Invitational Track Meet.

Off the playing field, White Spot supports many other youth-related programs. At Science World, a non-profit educational centre, both Dinosaurs! A Journey Through Time With White Spot, held during the summer of 1988, and Muppets, Monsters and Magic, from May to September of 1992, received extensive financial support from White Spot, as well as in-restaurant promotions of these two entertaining exhibits. The Pirate Pak, the restaurant's all-time favourite kid's meal, was even redesigned and renamed the Muppet Pak for the 1992 display.

Moreover, in 1993, White Spot initiated an annual scholarship for deserving students of Vancouver Community College's Hospitality Administration program. Peter Toigo established the endowment to honour the late, respected Vancouverite, Louis Stervinou, a dashing Frenchman and a superb restaurateur, whom Peter asked in the early 1980s to join White Spot. With consummate skill and great personal warmth, Louis directed the food services at Expo 86 for Nat Bailey's on the Plaza and the acclaimed Galleria. It is in his memory that the Louis Stervinou Scholarship was created.

White Spot also takes great pride in helping with the many programs, events and institutions, both local and national, which make such a difference to the quality of life in British Columbia. The list is a long one, including donations to the White Spot Pipe Band and Highland Dancers, the United Way, Variety Club Telethon, Timmy's Christmas Telethon and the Children's Miracle Network Telethon. And the support is not only financial. At many a telethon, White Spot has contributed the behind-the-scenes catering for the volunteers, while the people answering the telephones may well be White Spot staff. At Seafest '93, the Vancouver sea festival, a portion of the proceeds from the food sold by White Spot's mobile trailer, "Triple-O on the Go," were donated to the non-profit B.C. Sports Hall of Fame Museum.

Having operated drive-in restaurants for 65 years, promoting driver safety is also a top priority with White Spot. Since the late 1980s, the company has given away tens of thousands of "If You Drink, Don't Drive" bumper and window stickers, making the slogan a by-word with B.C. drivers.

In the community, in schools, institutions and even on the road, White Spot has long played a role in the well-being of British Columbia. It's a tradition that reflects the pride in every neighbourhood it calls home.

• White Spot has always been associated with the automobile, and actively promotes safety on the road.

The Great Fire

It was a rainy Friday, February 7, 1986, when the original White Spot at Granville and 67th burned down, taking with it art and artifacts, kitchen equipment, and above all, nearly 50 years of memories. Sadly, just seven years before, the combination drive-in, restaurant and dining room had been extensively renovated. In keeping with the overall Victorian look, designer Earl Morrison had added stained glass panels, including the Singleton windows, dating from London in the 1400s. Care was especially taken to preserve the log cabin facade, and no structural changes were made.

As eight fire engines rushed to quell the blaze which began above the kitchen, flames tore through the building's shingle roof, leaving only the log walls standing.

One of the city's most beloved buildings, White Spot #1 was more than a restaurant to the people who had grown up with it. As it burned beyond repair, crowds stood on the street with tears in their eyes. Rush-hour traffic in south Vancouver came to a halt, and for a month afterwards, a solemn procession of cars passed through the deserted parking lot. Thousands more called White Spot's head office to express their sympathy at the loss. A good friend was gone and an era had come to an end.

• **A 48-year-old gem is destroyed in a day as flames outrace firefighters trying to save White Spot #1.**

• It's only fitting that a White Spot team would be baseball champions. The 1989 White Spot Legends won their league title.

properties across British Columbia, building a hotel in Vancouver (now the Quality Inn), another in Barriere, north of Kamloops, and purchasing hotels in Clearwater, Revelstoke, Port Alberni and elsewhere.

Throughout the 1970s, Peter was engaged in several different business ventures. At one point in the mid-1970s, he was on the brink of personal bankruptcy. But instead of accepting defeat, he climbed out of debt, repaying his creditors 100 percent on every dollar owed. His entrepreneurial spirit, the principles of his youth and the encouragement of his wife always kept him going.

By the time General Foods was ready to sell White Spot, Peter was ready to buy. Immediately after the purchase, he hired Peter T. Main as president and CEO of White Spot Limited. Main's appointment marked the start of the most aggressive development program in the company's history. The new president was well acquainted with White Spot: he had been with General Foods, Limited since 1969, and was president of White Spot Limited between 1973 and 1978.

Main's experience and sensitivity to White Spot's reputation was instrumental in pulling the company through its darkest hours in the late summer of 1985, when an outbreak of botulism struck one White Spot location. Afterwards, White Spot worked closely with Vancouver's chief health officer, Dr. John Blatherwick, who praised the company for its co-operation in providing food ingredients and information for lab analysis. The results of the health officer's two-month-long research pointed to

More than Meets the Eye

Simple success is more complicated than it looks. In addition to its 39 restaurants, White Spot Limited encompasses four operating divisions: ICL Services Division, its food and beverage management company; the B.C. Complex Division (including the private British Columbia Club as well as catering services for Enterprise Hall, both located on the former Expo 86 site); Winchell's Eatery, an informal café serving high quality food; and the Granville House commissary.

Of these, ICL Services was the first to join. Its founder, Bill Tuson, brought the company into the White Spot fold in 1959. The ICL logo now appears at many events and institutions across British Columbia, from Douglas College to the Whistler Conference Centre, making it the largest business of its type in the province. ICL Services has also helped develop food and beverage facilities for the Vancouver Canucks, Edmonton Oilers, Pittsburgh Penguins and Kamloops Blazers and provides liquor service for the Vancouver Canucks in their Centre Ice Club, Gallery Suites, Press Gallery and Directors' Lounge.

The British Columbia Club

A Summit Experience

While running two restaurants at Expo 86, White Spot found itself literally in the centre of Vancouver's World Exposition. And what an exciting place to be! From the day that British Columbia's then-premier Bill Bennett asked White Spot to open the B.C. Pavilion's signature restaurant, Nat Bailey's on the Plaza, as well as the elegant Galleria above it for private parties, it was full speed ahead for Peter C. Toigo and his White Spot staff.

Hour-long line-ups were commonplace at Nat Bailey's, located on the popular Plaza of Nations, the hub of Expo's local and international activities. But once inside, the wait was worth it. The restaurant proved to be the calm in a busy sea of Expo visitors.

Today, White Spot is still on the Plaza of Nations with the British Columbia Club. A private facility for business professionals, the B.C. Club is more than 17,000 square feet in size. Members enjoy a haute cuisine dining room and lounge, meeting rooms and business and secretarial support. Throughout the year, the club hosts major events such as the Molson Indy, the International Dragon Boat Festival, B.C. Lions' home games, the Home Show and the Vancouver Sea Festival.

Few occasions, however, have demanded as much careful attention to detail as the U.S. Presidential Luncheon Cruise during the recent 1993 Summit. On the upper deck of the Orca Spirit, President Bill Clinton and an intimate party of 56 others dined on B.C. salmon, Queen Charlotte halibut and bison roast. On the lower deck, 130 more from the White House and Russian press corps enjoyed a similar repast. As the ship cruised up Indian Arm, chef Jean Pierre Guerin was rightfully proud of the British Columbia Club's sumptuous buffet presentation. With less than a week's notice, the White Spot division had staged a major culinary coup. "The people on board told us it was the best food they'd had the whole time they were here," said Jean Pierre. And as the Orca Spirit swung about to return to port, Jean Pierre could be satisfied that summit professionals had given White Spot very high marks. "I guess we were a hit with the U.S. Secret Service as well — we even sent samples to them for their approval." A compliment to the chef indeed!

- U.S. President Bill Clinton is welcomed aboard the *Orca Spirit* by B.C. Club chef Jean Pierre Guerin (right foreground).

• *Below right:* Take-out menus change with the times — 1993 (left) and 1970 (right). *Below left:* White Spot offers its guests the chance to win a classic vehicle. *Right:* Richmond Centre White Spot staff members were awarded colour television sets by Peter Toigo in 1992 for their overall excellence in service.

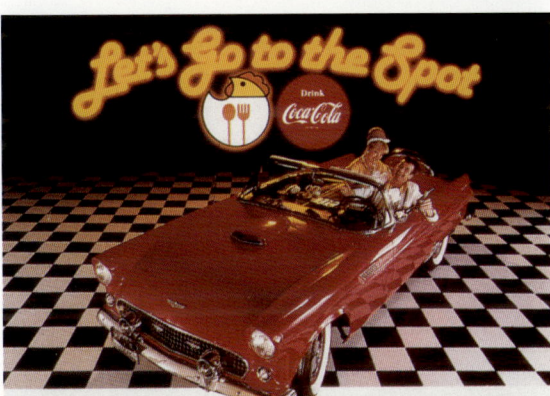

Portrait of a Franchise

Michele Metcalfe, the 26-year-old co-owner and manager of the 156-seat Vernon White Spot — the first franchised White Spot in the company's history — followed her parents into the food industry. In October 1987, she was hired as a server at White Spot in Kelowna; by 1988, she had moved up to management. Later, she was called on by White Spot to assist with openings at Richmond Centre and Kamloops before returning to Kelowna as general manager.

In 1992, White Spot purchased a site in the Vernon Square Shopping Centre for a future restaurant. Next the company did some matchmaking, introducing Michele to Claude and Carole Zorzi of Newmarket, Ontario, who wanted to become silent partners in a White Spot franchise. Soon Michele was convinced of the merits of the new enterprise. In addition to helping her with every aspect of the opening, White Spot totally renovated and redecorated the new restaurant in the company's 1990s' "French Country" look. Guests are seated in comfortable oak booths, swagged with cloth valances for more privacy. The look is replete with floral patterns in rose, green and purple, with overhead shelves dotted with artifacts.

Before opening the Vernon restaurant, Michele invited a group of local people to dine as her guests so that her trainees could work with real customers. As a result, the opening went surprisingly smoothly. Like any other White Spot, recalled Michele, it was extremely busy from day one, but the weeks of staff training paid off. The new co-owner continues to be just as busy: one day she's up to her elbows making fresh strawberry pie, another she's working with accounting and payroll, which before were "magically done by White Spot."

"One of my employees asked me, 'Did you know this is what you always wanted to do?'" recounted Michele. "I could reply honestly that I enjoy working with my staff and meeting the guests. I really love my job and I love working with White Spot. They're wonderful people, the best."

• Working with the best: Michele Metcalfe (left foreground) celebrates the opening of her White Spot franchise in Vernon with partners Claude and Carole Zorzi.

an imported garlic spread and nothing made by White Spot. The outbreak was ultimately viewed by Dr. Blatherwick as "a freak thing," and soon the company had won back the trust of its loyal customers.

During the 1980s, the catering division had grown and Kentucky Fried Chicken had expanded to virtually every community throughout the province. White Spot was a neighbourhood presence not only in Greater Vancouver but in Kelowna, Abbotsford, Nanaimo and Victoria. The company's commissary alone was one of the largest food-manufacturing operations in western Canada.

Two other landmark projects were connected with Expo 86, Vancouver's 1986 World Exposition. Appointed as the host restaurant at the B.C. Pavilion, White Spot opened a 325-seat restaurant, Nat Bailey's on the Plaza. It proved to be a sell-out success, with crowds often waiting more than an hour to get a table. A second Expo venture, The Galleria, was also managed by White Spot. Located on the third floor above Nat Bailey's, The Galleria hosted visiting dignitaries, including Prince Charles, Princess Diana, Princess Margaret and George Bush, then vice-president of the United States.

As White Spot Limited entered the 1990s, a new strength and new vision was emerging. Staff and management across British Columbia committed themselves to "Being the Best," both as a mission statement and as a promise to their guests. Service had never been faster or friendlier and many of the restaurants had a fresh new look. For the first time, White Spot introduced franchising as an option, celebrating the opening of its first franchise, in Vernon, B.C., in March 1993. As well, a significant move was made into the U.S. market with the launch of a Bellingham, Washington White Spot Restaurant.

From Nat Bailey, White Spot inherited pride in its menu and a respect for its guests. From General Foods, it gained modern business procedures and marketing approaches. Today, Peter Toigo's White Spot combines the best of these worlds, making it a fitting monument both to Nat's original dream and Peter's ongoing drive for innovation and excellence. •

• Peter Toigo, like Nat Bailey before him, exemplifies the qualities that continue to make White Spot a success: high standards, innovation and personal commitment. Here, Peter is the genial host to a counterful of guests.

Nothing Else Tastes Like White Spot

good ideas for new menu items come from many sources, thanks in part to inveterate traveller Peter C. Toigo. After meeting famed Executive Chef Nicholas Klontz of California's Pritikin Longevity Centre, Peter wanted to develop a menu to meet with the criteria of the Heart and Stroke Foundation's Heart Smart Restaurant Program. Nicholas Klontz was brought to Vancouver to consult with White Spot's food and beverage manager, and as a result, guests could choose from low-fat, low-sodium dishes such as Fettuccine Primavera and Penne with Italian Sausage. "We don't just wake up to something new," Peter recalled. "It takes real work to create items that appeal to a wide range of tastes and dietary needs."

Behind the scenes, every new dish considered by White Spot goes through a vigorous approval process. First, the concept is scrutinized by the Product Development Committee's dozen members, including restaurant managers and staff from the Food and Beverage, Purchasing, Marketing and Operations departments. Then the proposed dish goes to the test kitchen, where ingredients are chosen, a recipe created, and samples sent to half a dozen White Spot locations for guests to sample. If the dish meets the approval of diners and can also meet White Spot's standards of taste, quality and price, it will appear as a permanent fixture on the menu. When the use of cod, for example, was restricted by the Canadian government, White Spot had a number of choices available and as a result of thorough testing, the Product Development Committee chose premium west coast halibut, rather than sole or flounder, as the best possible alternative.

Not every great idea, though, makes it on White Spot's menu. One of Peter Toigo's great regrets was Spaghetti Pie, "the one that got away." Introduced to the unique dish in Phoenix, Arizona, Peter sent two of his senior staff members from Vancouver to try it out. Approval was unanimous, and Spaghetti Pie seemed destined for White Spot guests. Unfortunately, the pie's ingredients made it impossible to prepare fresh on a daily basis. "Sometimes things happen that way," sighed Peter, "but I still haven't given up on Spaghetti Pie."

Heart Smart

• In 1993, to commemorate its 65th year, White Spot offered its guests newly designed menus with sumptuous choices for morning, noon and night-time dining.

Hospitality Has No Borders

expansion down the north-south corridor seemed a natural move for the company. The strategy was confirmed by market research, which showed that Bellingham was an excellent place to open the first White Spot outside B.C. There was considerable White Spot name recognition in the Bellingham area from Vancouver television advertising and Expo 86, when major marketing programs spotlighted Vancouver. Many U.S. visitors had suggested at the time that the company expand into the States.

The idea looked promising, but there were obstacles: a family company in Denver had the patent for the White Spot name in the United States and was operating two White Spot restaurants there. British Columbia White Spot management went to Denver to negotiate and bought the name and U.S. licence from the family.

Although Bellingham is close to the Canadian border, it was a whole new world for White Spot. Focus groups were held with 20 Bellingham residents at the White Spot in White Rock to consider menu and decor. Among other things, White Spot learned that Americans preferred larger pieces of fish in their fish 'n' chips and didn't use much white vinegar. The Americans also wanted Mexican food. As a result, the Bellingham menu includes Santa Fe Salad, Mexican Omelette and Quesadillas.

One fervent admirer of the new franchise is Ray Smith, chairman of the Board of MacMillan Bloedel. "I've been to the new Bellingham outlet three times now and I'll go back again many times," reported Ray. In fact, it's fair to say that as far as cross-border trade goes, Canadian hospitality travels exceptionally well. "It's a real White Spot with its dedication to service and quality. They really got it right. The quality that Nat Bailey established is still there, no question about that."

• Familiar surroundings in a foreign locale: the interior of the Bellingham, Washington restaurant – White Spot's first location in the U.S.

• *Above:* The North Vancouver location, opened in 1989, welcomes busy shoppers and movie-goers to the Park and Tilford Centre. *Right:* A family enjoys Pirate Paks at one of White Spot's most popular locations, Granville and Broadway.

"I was born in B.C. and my mother worked for White Spot for 35 years. My personal connection goes way back to 1956 when I started at CJOR and White Spot was one of my sponsors. I was 16 years old at the time and my show was the first radio show in Canada dedicated to rock 'n' roll. In 1987, White Spot gave away a red 1957 Thunderbird as part of the promotion for my Rock 'n' Roll Reunion show at the Coliseum. In six weeks, the company received 460,000 entries. It was remarkable.

"When Peter Toigo took over White Spot, he recognized the company's historical significance and brought it back to life. My full marks go to him. He's here, he's a local, he's one of us."

— **Red Robinson,** Red Robinson Management Ltd.

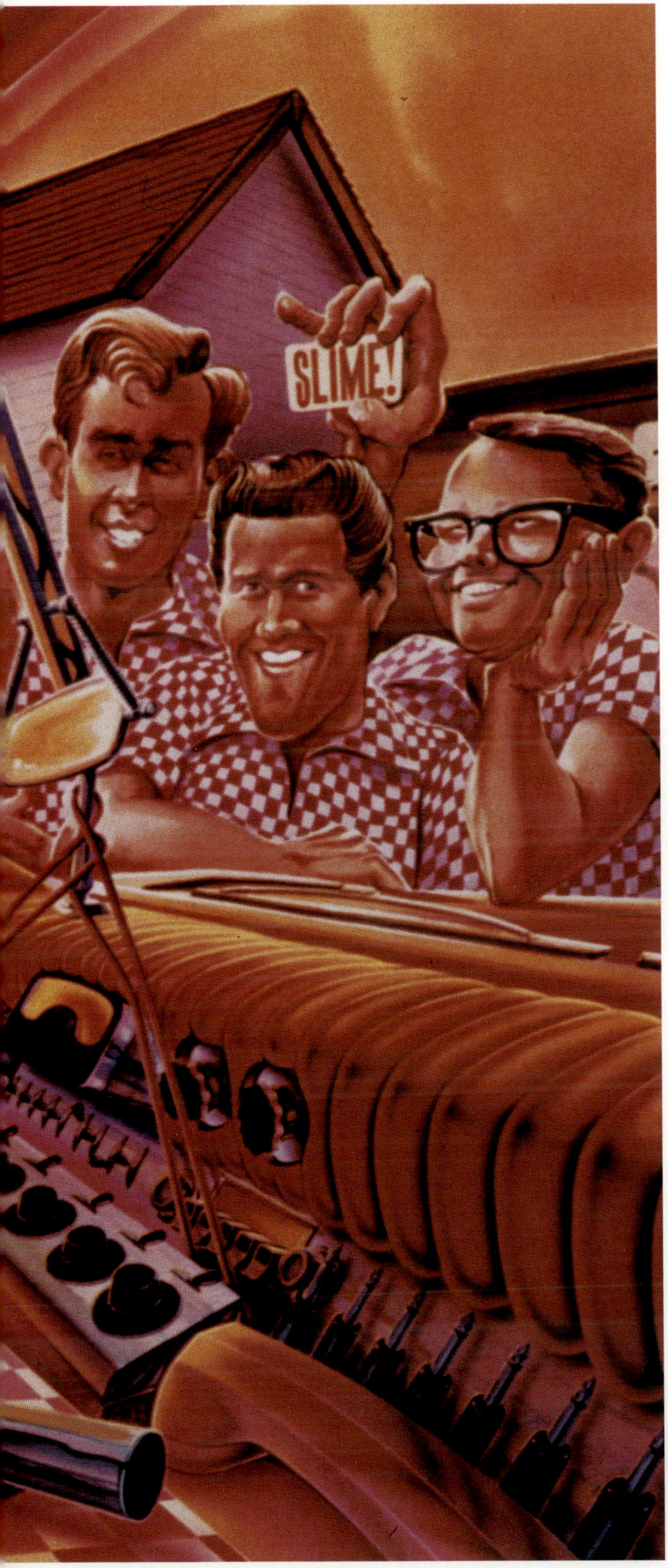

COURTESY OF RED ROBINSON

COURTESY OF RED ROBINSON

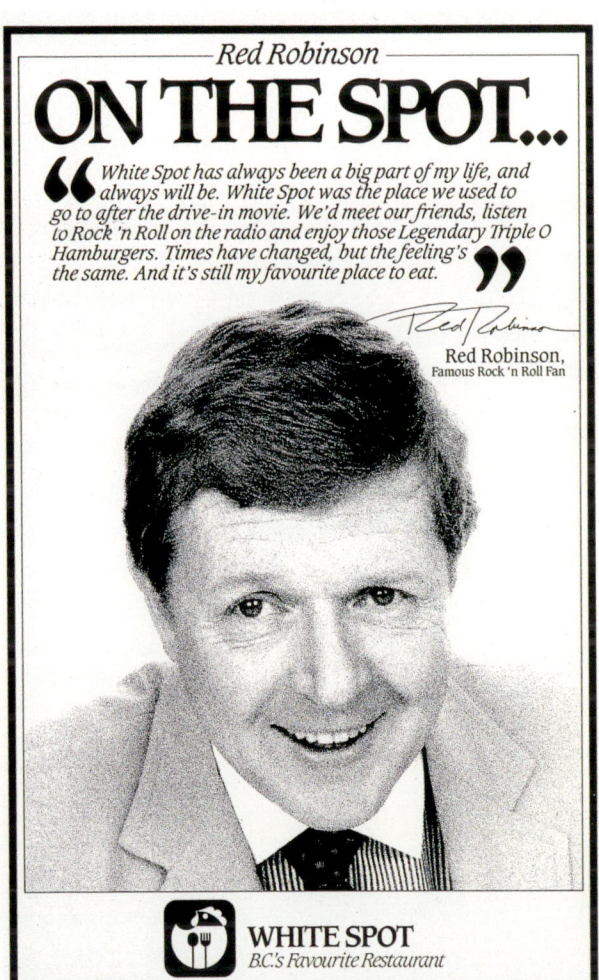

• ***Left:*** **Artist Bruce Stewart's illustration for Red Robinson's 50th birthday – Red as a young DJ, cruising White Spot with local radio colleagues (left to right): wife Carole Robinson, Red, Tom Peacock, Frosty Forst, Fred Latremouille, Ed Kargl, Al Jordan.** ***Above:*** **The White Spot celebrities ad campaign featuring Red Robinson.**

White Spot Memories

I was born and raised out here. I remember going to White Spot a long time ago in very short pants and very old cars over to the original Drive-in with its menus up on what looked like huge outdoor billboards. When I was four years old, they made a big impression on me. We all knew the legend of Nat Bailey selling peanuts in the ball concessions. It adds up to good community memories.

"I've watched White Spot go through its changes to its present corporate status. I still like it, especially the Triple-O burger and double chocolate milkshake. I really love that food. They have also done a great job on their new look."

— **Fred Latremouille,** broadcaster, 97 KISS FM

• **Fred Latremouille**

"I went to school in Marpole so I remember Nat Bailey from the very early days, more than 65 years ago. He used to bag peanuts in the basement of the building where my father worked. On weekends, I'd be up on the fourth floor with my father and I'd drop a long string with a paper-clip attached down the side of the building to Nat. He'd attach a bag of peanuts and then I'd pull it up. Later, as a teenager, I worked at the Colonial Theatre and would have lunch at Purdy's. Eva worked in the restaurant there and we became friends. I remember when she told us she was going to marry Nat, we were all so happy for her."

— **Hugh Picket,** impresario

"The truth is, White Spot is far more to British Columbia than a chain of restaurants. It's part of the culture of the province. Over the years, it has become part of personal friendships, too. That was best demonstrated at Expo 86, at Nat Bailey's on the Plaza. The opening was Mr. Toigo's first public handshake with the city. Every mover and shaker was on hand; it was a marvellous celebration and showed without a doubt his dedication to the history of White Spot and his respect for the founder."

— **Gary Bannerman,** broadcaster, writer

"My introduction to White Spot was in 1974. For ten years, I used to eat out at the Park Royal restaurant with other team members from the Whitecaps. These days I'm over there about twice a week, with my wife and our two kids. They like the Pirate Paks and I like the fact that the coffee is always hot. It's affordable and we particularly enjoy the family atmosphere."

— **Bob Lenarduzzi,** coach, Canadian National Soccer Team; general manager and head coach, Vancouver Eighty-Sixers Soccer Team

"I moved to B.C. from Alberta when I was 13, but it wasn't until I was an adult that I had my first White Spot experience. About 12 years ago, my wife Jennifer took me to the White Spot in Coquitlam. She said I had to order a Legendary Hamburger with Triple-O sauce and I had to have it the way she liked hers — with raw onions. I thought she was putting me on, but, no, she went ahead and ordered raw onions for both of us. Sure enough, it was great, and it's now my favourite, too.

When new team-mates come to Vancouver, I send them to White Spot; it's one of the better family restaurants. I take my family there regularly, to the drive-in at Park Royal. My three kids get a kick out of walking up to the carhop window to place their orders. Then they come back to the car and wait for the trays to arrive."

— **Stan Smyl,** assistant coach, Vancouver Canucks

• Stan Smyl

"When the new menu came out this past New Year's, I discovered to my dismay that my favourite Hot Turkey Sandwich was no longer offered. 'That's impossible,' I said and called over the waiter who confirmed the bad news. So I did an editorial on CKNW addressed to Mr. Toigo, asking him to please put it back on the menu. White Spot got so many calls that they decided to bring it back. A little table announcement soon appeared telling customers they could still order the item. I was overjoyed!"

— **Joy Metcalfe,** CKNW

"I started doing the Owl Prowl on CKNW back in 1947 and from 1948 into the 1950s, I did radio commercials for White Spot. Because drive-ins were the place to be in those days, I'd say something like: 'Okay, gang, where are you now? Down in Stanley Park?' Later on, around 1954, my wife and I did television commercials for White Spot, dressed up in staff uniforms and ad-libbing our lines. I knew Nat Bailey during those years and I remember him as a prince of a guy. We all had a lot of fun in those early years."

— **Jack Cullen,** broadcaster, CKNW

"When I first came to Vancouver from the Prairies, everyone told me I had to try "The Spot" right away. Their tone was reverent, as if it was my patriotic duty, so I went and I was convinced. Years later, I hosted a two-hour radio show in White Spot's honour. We started with breakfast at 6 A.M. at Georgia and Seymour and dozens of celebrities came by, including the mayor and many media and sports figures. It was awesome. A million people showed up for breakfast, including owner Peter Toigo. He laughed and thanked us all but he was too shy to go on the air."

— **Rick Honey,** broadcaster, CKNW

Epilogue   The Legend Continues

Sixty-five years after it began, White Spot's commitment to its guests, good food and friendly service has won it countless friends. From the very first breakfasts served at 6:30 A.M. through to lunch, dinner and late-night snacks, White Spot ensures that the food will be fresh and delicious. Equally important, the ambience will be warm and inviting. There's always a friendly face at the reception desk and a smile at your table, both rare commodities in a world dominated by fast-food and faster turnovers. Above and beyond the practical concerns of prompt service and affordability there is an indescribable White Spot "feeling" that continues to draw people back time and again.

When you sit in a White Spot, you're at home. The staff is friendly, not fawning; the service efficient, not rushed. Care and concern for guests is evident everywhere, in the big and small touches that make this family restaurant stand out above the others: the personal way a host or hostess escorts you to your seat, booths that are private and cosy, and breakfasts available at any hour of the day. "We changed our approach to our customers and began to think of them as guests," says owner Peter C. Toigo. "And we want each one of them to say, 'That was outstanding, and we'll be back.'"

Every effort is made to ensure just that. Indeed, pleasing its guests is a tradition with White Spot that started with founder Nat Bailey. Where Nat offered barbecued roast beef, chicken and veal sandwiches, White Spot now has over 120 items on its menus.

As it approaches a new century, White Spot is proud of its many accomplishments and determined to continue building on them. Whether adding new restaurants or renovating existing ones, assisting franchises or making inroads into the U.S. market, the company's vision for the 1990s, "Being the Best," guides its every action.

The process of creating this vision began three years ago. Recalls Peter Toigo, "As a company we were so well known that it would have been easy to pat ourselves on the back and say what an excellent job we were doing. But that wasn't good enough for us. We decided to develop a vision based on our successes and our belief that we want to be the customer's first choice every time." White Spot set a course so that employees and management could all work together to take a fresh look at its operations.

Over a period of six months, senior management took to the road to consult with staff at each location. Every aspect of the company, from service standards to the bottom line, was discussed and debated. As a result of this process, White Spot found that its employees, wherever they worked in British Columbia, genuinely believed in the company. Together, staff and management developed a set of goals they could aspire to achieve and agreed to measure progress through guest assessment, research, analysis and employee feedback.

In everyday terms, "Being the Best," means putting guest satisfaction at the top of the priority list. The length of time you have to wait for a table, the promptness of food delivery and even the friendly smile of your server have all come under careful scrutiny to ensure that guests are completely satisfied with their dining experience. The company retains its

• **Facing page:** White Spot embraces generations: Peter Toigo enjoys an Expo 86 celebration at Nat Bailey's on the Plaza with grandson Michael Green.

loyal and enthusiastic following by practising the five values it has chosen for itself — accountability, innovation, teamwork, trust and pride.

White Spot has maintained its strong reputation and made refinements to please more of its guests more of the time. It introduced the biggest menu changes in its history, including separate menus for different segments of the day. "We asked them what they wanted to see on our menus and how they wanted to be treated by our staff. We even hired 'mystery shoppers' who posed as diners and then reported on how we were doing," says Peter Toigo of the ongoing process. As a reflection of the company's intense efforts, a recent Angus Reid poll reported that White Spot is now number one for quality and value, friendly and fast service, and menu variety. It is also the most popular breakfast stop in the province and at lunch, is second only to McDonald's — all positive proof that the new vision is taking the company in the right direction: forward.

"Being the Best" also means creating the best place for employees to work, from fleet drivers to food preparers, office assistants to location managers. In a demanding industry, personal fulfillment and satisfaction are imperative if employees are going to make a commitment to being the best at their jobs. Over the years, White Spot has been proud of its many longtimers — staff of more than 10, 20 and even 40 years. To ensure this kind of continued loyalty, the company offers wages, benefits and working conditions that make it the industry leader. Many a busboy or server has worked his or her way up into management, a tenet of the White Spot credo from the very start.

Two other major moves are also important to the future of the company. In 1993, White Spot introduced the first of its franchise locations, in Vernon, B.C. This new restaurant, run with care and commitment, offers the same fine food and efficient service as any location. Franchising has allowed White Spot to move into smaller market areas, supported by the entrepreneurial spirit of local, hard-working people like Michele Metcalfe, co-owner and manager of the Vernon franchise.

White Spot, as well, is exploring the American market, a program that began in 1993 with the opening of its first U.S. restaurant in Bellingham, Washington. The new location brings Canadian style and tradition to American customers. In return, B.C. residents are destined to enjoy popular

south-of-the-border menu items, such as Mexican Quesadillas and Santa Fe Salad. New high quality food centres, such as the Winchell's Eatery located next door to the Bellingham restaurant, as well as take-out bakery counters at White Spot locations like the Oakridge Mall, are also being added to the company mix.

In 1928, only two employees worked at the White Spot Barbecue, one as a cook, the other as a carhop serving hot dogs and sandwiches to drivers parked on the gravel lot. By 1935, in the midst of the Depression, staff had increased to a dozen employees, most of whom worked their way up from washing dishes or sweeping floors to carhopping at the drive-in. Wages were low compared to today's standards, but greatly appreciated at a time when employment, particularly for young single men, was almost impossible to find. A teenage coffee boy at White Spot, bringing home 25 cents an hour, made a big difference to his family's security. Today White Spot's staff has climbed to more than 3,200 people, making it one of British Columbia's largest employers.

The first day's revenue, back in 1928, was less than $10, with a mere handful of customers trying out the unique new drive-in. Today, White Spot serves more than 35,000 guests daily. That adds up to more than 13 million people a year, the equivalent of half of Canada. Some part of White Spot's operation has direct, face-to-face contact with one-third of all British Columbian families each and every week. The restaurant group now includes 39 locations as well as several additional operating divisions.

The number of anniversaries, birthdays, first dates, graduations, business deals and even marriages celebrated over a Triple-O at "The Spot" will never be known. But without a doubt, the love affair between the 65-year-old restaurant and its guests continues. And the pace is certainly not slackening. The restaurant family is still growing and still setting new goals and challenges for itself. In the words of Peter Toigo, "White Spot started with the enterprising spirit of Nat Bailey's days. We haven't lost that energy even though we now have locations throughout B.C. as well as the U.S. The way I look at it, we're not just celebrating the first 65 years of White Spot but the next 65 as well. In every way, this is just the beginning." •

• A 65th anniversary ad features representative employees from all Lower Mainland locations, gathered together for a portrait of the White Spot family of 1993.

Acknowledgements

Opus Productions would like to extend special thanks to the management and staff of White Spot who provided their generous assistance on this project.

Chairman, Shato Holdings Limited: Peter C. Toigo
Senior Vice-President, Shato Holdings Limited: Peter R. Toigo
President, White Spot Limited: Dale Parker
Division General Manager: Warren Erhart
Marketing Coordinator: Louise Hendrickson
Marketing Assistant: Chiyoko Kakino

Opus Productions is grateful to the following people for their invaluable assistance in providing archival material and historical information:

Bob Stout, Erwin Jellen, Mark and Ryan Andrews

Opus Productions would like to thank the following individuals and institutions for their contributions to this project.

Amir Mulji • Bill Senghera • Bob Lenarduzzi • Bob Faulkner, Metropolitan Press • VRH Communications: Brian Follett, Pat Busswood, David Sandor, Graham Livingstone, Barry Lyman, Louise Buckmaster • Brian Loney • Bruce Darby, Jennifer McCallum, Judy Bau, Chris Dahl Art &Design •

Carmella Toigo • Carol Haber, Janette MacDougall, City of Vancouver Archives • David Ker, Rotary Club of Vancouver South • Debra Costanzo • Denise Buchanan • Derik Murray Photography Inc. • Devin Francis Murray • Don Bellamy • Ernie Creamer • Frank Krische • Fred Latremouille • Gary Bannerman • George Mittlestead • Geraldine Cooper • Fair and Helen Fawcett • Hugh Pickett • Jack Cullen • Jack Diamond • Jagtar Nijjar • Jan Westendorp • Jeff Parkinson • Jennifer Nelson • Jim Pattison • Joe Mandarino • Joy Metcalfe • Karen Grey • Karen Love • Linda Swartos • Laurie Robertson, Vancouver Public Library Historic Photographs • Michele Metcalfe • Millie Wylie • Myee Lindmayer, B.C. Club • Norene Kimberley • Pat Armstrong, Cheryl McNeil, B.C. Sports Hall of Fame and Museum • Paul Wylie • Peggy Parkinson • Peter Main • Peter Bancroft • Phil Bayley • Red Robinson • Rick Honey • Robert Lyons • Robert W. Hiller • Roland McGee • Roy Parkinson • Sandy Arthur • Sharon Berry, KISS FM • Stan Smyl • Steve MacIntyre • Steve Fee • Teresa Evans • Total Graphics • Waterford Communications • Wilf Trice

Opus Productions would like to thank the following local sources for assistance in providing selected props appearing in photographs throughout this book.

Aileen's Antiques • Empress Antiques • Gasoline Alley • Kelly's Collection • Memory Lane • Old Stuff Two • Old Friends Antiques • R2B2 Books • Red Barn Antiques • Salmagundi West

Bibliography

Andrews, Mark. Personal interview. May, 1993.

Andrews, Ryan. Personal interview. June, 1993.

"Bailey buys out eastern food outlets." *The Vancouver Sun*. June 10, 1959.

Baldrey, Keith. "White Spot workers to rally". *The Vancouver Sun*. September 30, 1985.

Bannerman, Gary. Telephone interview. May, 1993.

Bayley, Phil. Telephone interview. May, 1993.

Beddoes, Dick. *The Vancouver Sun*. February 8, 1961.

Bellamy, Don. Telephone interview. May, 1993.

—. *White Spot pipe band and highland dancers: Brief history*. May 4, 1993.

Boyd, Denny. "The legend of Triple-O lives on." *The Vancouver Sun*. February 25, 1980.

—. "Like a burger from ashes, the White Spot rises again." *The Vancouver Sun*. September 24, 1986.

Bradford, Earl. *Earl's Court with Earl Bradford*. CKNW. December 9, 1985.

Brini, Domenic. Telephone interview. May, 1993

—. *The history of Pacific Coast League baseball in Vancouver*. BCIT student thesis. April 26, 1978.

Clancy, William. Telephone interview. May, 1993.

Cooper, Geraldine. Telephone interview. May, 1993.

Costanzo, Debra. Telephone interview. May, 1993.

Cox, Sarah. "Owner cooks up development plan for burned restaurant site." *The Vancouver Sun*. June 18, 1986.

Creamer, Ernie. Telephone interview. May, 1993.

Cullen, Jack. Telephone interview. July, 1993.

Davis, Chuck. *Reflections: One hundred years*. Vancouver: Opus Productions Inc., 1990.

Diamond, Jack. Telephone interview. May, 1993.

Evans, Teresa. Telephone interviews. May, 1993.

Fawcett, Fair. Telephone interview. April, 1993.

Fawcett, Helen. Telephone interview. April, 1993.

GF Canadian. Multiple issues. 1968 - 1981.

Gourley, Cathie. "White Spot is moving up in the world." *The Province*. January 5, 1977.

Grant, Sheilah. Telephone interview. June, 1993.

Grey, Karen. Telephone interview. June, 1993.

"Hamburger king Bailey's peanuts-to-riches life ends at 76." *The Vancouver Sun*. March 28, 1978.

"Hamburger's entrepreneur." *The Province*. July 9, 1965.

Hiller, Robert W. Telephone interview. June, 1993.

Honey, Rick. Telephone interview. July, 1993.

Katin, Louis. "Nat Bailey of the White Spot." Publication unknown, December, 1955.

Kearney, Jim. "Champions." Publication unknown, 1985.

Ker, David. Telephone interview. May, 1993.

Kluckner, Michael. *Vancouver, the way it was*. Vancouver: Whitecap Books Ltd., 1984.

Kreiser, Vince. *Vancouver's legacy of recreation facilities*. Vancouver Community College. Fall, 1990.

Krische, Frank. Telephone interviews. June, 1993.

Larsen, Bruce. "City group ready to buy Mounties." *The Vancouver Sun*. November 8, 1960.

—. "City syndicate willing to bail out Mounties." *The Vancouver Sun*. September 23, 1961.

—. "$40,000 in a hurry or Mounties fold." *The Vancouver Sun*. February 8, 1961.

—. "Mounties sale off – re-finance or fold." *The Vancouver Sun*. October 20, 1960.

Latremouille, Fred. Telephone interview. June, 1993.

Lekich, John. "My Vancouver, my life." *Vancouver magazine*. December, 1992.

Lenarduzzi, Bob. Telephone interview. July, 1993.

"Long-time CRA member now heads B.C. region." *Dogwood Trails*. March, 1972.

Loranger, Clancy. "Many people will miss the peanut hustler." *The Province*. March 28, 1978.

—. "Mounties acquire directors." *The Province*. January 12, 1947.

Lytle, Andy. "Nat Bailey." (profile) *The Vancouver Sun Magazine Supplement*. June 21, 1951.

Macdonald, Bruce. *Vancouver: A visual history*. Vancouver: Talonbooks, 1992.

McGee, Roland. Telephone interview. May, 1993.

McKenzie, Art. *B.C. Magazine*. Saturday, July 9, 1955.

McPhedran, Kerry. Telephone interview. June, 1993.

Metcalfe, Joy. Telephone interview. May, 1993.

Metcalfe, Michele. Telephone interview. June, 1993.

"Mr. Baseball Nat Bailey dies at 77." *The Province*. March 28, 1978.

Mittlestead, George. Telephone interview. May, 1993.

Moore, Jack. "The brand new lovely old Granville House." *MacLean's Guide*. April 4-18, 1979.

"Nat Bailey again heads Mounties." *The Vancouver Sun*. February 23, 1960.

"Nat Bailey scholarship established." *B.C. Hotelman*. May, 1978.

"Nat Bailey starts new career." *The Vancouver Sun*. January 2, 1969.

"Nat Bailey's new Oakridge Room 'finest restaurant on the coast'." *The Vancouver Sun*. May 5, 1959.

"Nat to miss first meet in 34 years." *B.C. Hotelman*. May, 1978.

Parkinson, Peggy. Telephone interview. April, 1993.

Parkinson, Roy. Telephone interview. April, 1993.

Pattison, Jim. Telephone interview. June, 1993.

Perkins, Walter. Telephone interview. May, 1993.

Pickett, Hugh. Telephone interview. June, 1993.

"Purchase of Mounties okayed." *The Vancouver Sun*. December 5, 1956.

Raible, Garry. *Sports Comment*. CJOR-60. March 28, 1978.

Robinson, Red. Telephone interview. June, 1993.

Sanderson, Sandy. "Noted restaurateur Nat Bailey dies at 76." *Hospitality Canada*. April, 1978.

Scurfield, Dan. *B.C. Hotelman*. May, 1965.

"Shedding the fast food image." *Food Service & Hospitality*. September, 1980.

Sirotnik, Gareth. *Running tough: The story of Vancouver's Jack Diamond*. Vancouver: Diamond Family, 1988.

Smallman, Hal. "The success story of Vancouver's Nat Bailey." *Canadian Food Journal*. September, 1961.

Smyl, Stan. Telephone interview. July, 1993

Spratley, Louise. "Trays spark million dollar industry." *B.C. Hotelman*. June, 1967.

Stout, Bob. Personal interviews. April - July, 1993.

Straight, Hal. "Sport rays: Calling Nat Bailey." Publication and date unknown.

Tait, David. Telephone interview. May, 1993.

"That hits the Spot!" *The Vancouver Courier*. October 12, 1986.

Thomson, Jamie. "Nat Bailey, the story." *B.C. Sportsmagazine*. December 15, 1971.

"White Spot blackened." *The Province*. June 24, 1959.

"White Spot business bounces back." *The Vancouver Sun*. June 14, 1986.

"White Spot employees accept offer." *The Vancouver Sun*. August 22, 1975.

White Spot News. Multiple issues. November 1976–June 1988.

"White Spot plans big building." *The Province*. November 7, 1957.

"White Spot tells $3.5 million plan." *The Vancouver Sun*. March 25, 1969.

White Spot: 25 years serving fine food 1928-1953. Twenty-fifth anniversary menu, 1953.

Wilson, Mark. "White Spot tries growth recipes." *The Province*. December 2, 1970.

Wylie, Millie. Telephone interview. May, 1993.